THE
BOOK OF
SPACE
FACTS AND RECORDS

THE
BOOK OF
SPACE
FACTS AND RECORDS

Stuart Atkinson

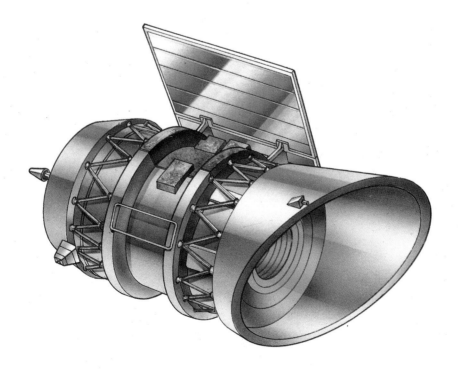

Derrydale
New York

First published in 1990 by Kingfisher Books
Copyright © Grisewood & Dempsey Ltd. 1990

This 1990 edition published by Derrydale Books,
distributed by Outlet Book Company, Inc.,
a Random House Company, 225 Park Avenue South,
New York, New York 10003.

Printed and bound in Spain
by Graficas Reunidas S.A., Madrid

ISBN 0-517-03051-9
8 7 6 5 4 3 2 1

INTRODUCTION

Today we are used to watching dramatic Space Shuttle blast-offs on television. The fact that it can carry men and women into orbit and back, again and again is taken for granted. But our conquest of space — and our understanding of the universe around us — has not just taken place over the last few decades. It has taken centuries to achieve. This book tells the amazing story of that conquest.

It describes how man has been fascinated by the universe around him ever since the first cave people gazed up at the stars glittering in the night sky. It describes how our knowledge of the Universe began to take shape with the invention of the telescope, and of early discoveries such as Galileo's first observations of Jupiter in 1610. Since then technology has given us bigger and better telescopes, and the satellites and computers which astronomers use to study and observe the universe around us.

After thousands of years staring up at the heavens it was only natural that we should reach out for those stars. This book will tell you how our conquest of space began with the launch of the very first artificial satellite — Sputnik 1 on October 4th, 1957. The satellite was just a tiny silver ball, but it was followed by much larger spacecraft. Soon men were circling the Earth. Yuri Gagarin's first flight was very short, but it was eventually to lead to men walking on the Moon, and living and working in space stations high above the Earth. Robot spaceprobes later explored and photographed worlds too distant for humans to reach. Learn about their incredible discoveries here, and about the exciting future plans to build bases and observatories on the Moon and send manned expeditions to Mars!

This book will take you on a journey of discovery through the past and on into the future. Enjoy the ride!

STUART ATKINSON

Contents

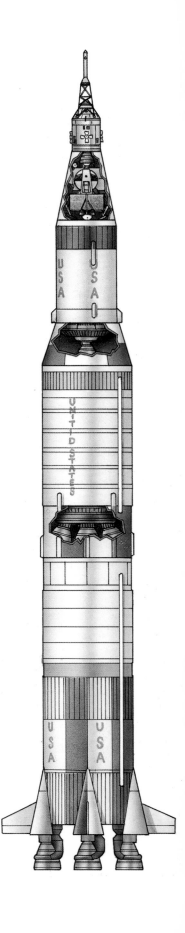

THE HEAVENS

SPACE TRAVEL

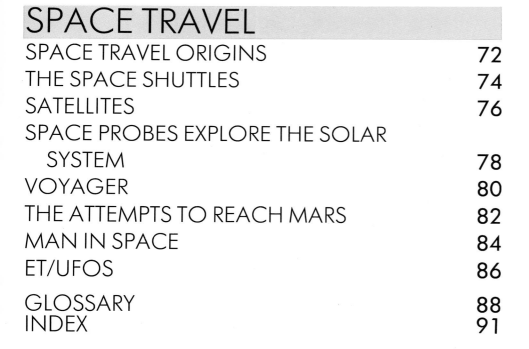

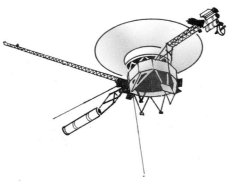

The Changing Views of the Universe

A medieval representation of Ptolemy

To the Egyptians, the heavens were their goddess Nut, while the Babylonians saw the Earth as a disk, surrounded by water and mountains.

To prehistoric people, the night sky was a huge animal hide, and stars tiny tears in the skin showing the fiery world of their gods.

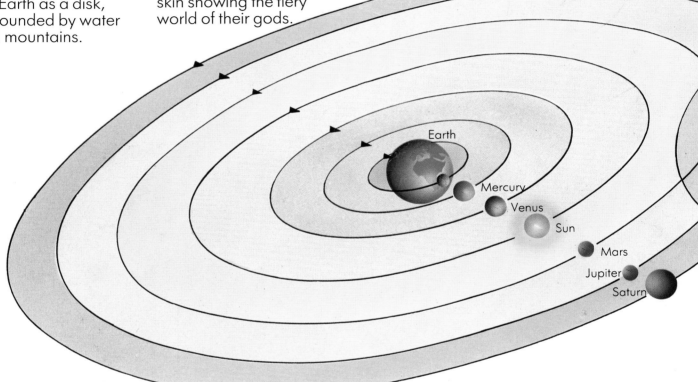

Earth
Mercury
Venus
Sun
Mars
Jupiter
Saturn

The Greek Pythagoras thought the Earth was a stationary spherical globe. Aristotle used mathematics to show that the Sun and planets moved around the Earth.

The Alexandrian researcher Ptolemy confirmed this view, and his Earth-centered Solar System was thus named the "Ptolemaic Universe" or "Ptolemaic System."

GALILEO

Years after Copernicus, an Italian scientist, Galileo Galilei, found proof of Copernicus's theory: Jupiter had four tiny "stars" spinning around it and Venus showed phases, changing from thin crescent to full disk. These phases could be explained only by Venus orbiting the Sun.

This discovery changed our view of the Universe for ever.

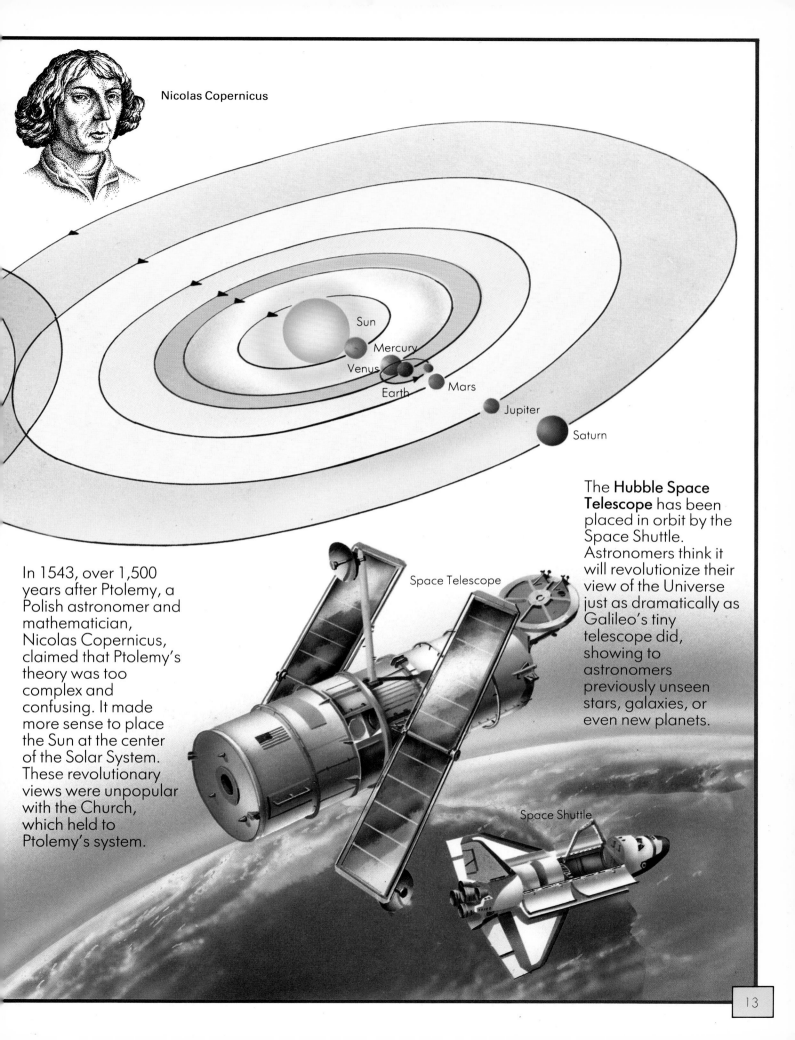

Nicolas Copernicus

Sun

Mercury

Venus

Earth

Mars

Jupiter

Saturn

In 1543, over 1,500 years after Ptolemy, a Polish astronomer and mathematician, Nicolas Copernicus, claimed that Ptolemy's theory was too complex and confusing. It made more sense to place the Sun at the center of the Solar System. These revolutionary views were unpopular with the Church, which held to Ptolemy's system.

Space Telescope

Space Shuttle

The **Hubble Space Telescope** has been placed in orbit by the Space Shuttle. Astronomers think it will revolutionize their view of the Universe just as dramatically as Galileo's tiny telescope did, showing to astronomers previously unseen stars, galaxies, or even new planets.

13

The Universe

The Universe is simply everything that exists. It is not just our Solar System and all the stars, galaxies and energy beyond it, but *everything* that exists anywhere. There are no limits to the Universe, although the size of telescopes limits how much we can observe from Earth. The Universe goes on and on for ever and ever. We think our Solar System is huge, and compared to the distance between the Earth and the Moon it is, but compared to the Universe, it is millions of times less important than one single cell in the massive body of a whale.

Planets

Mercury

Stars

Venus

Earth

Mars

Sun

Jupiter

Sa

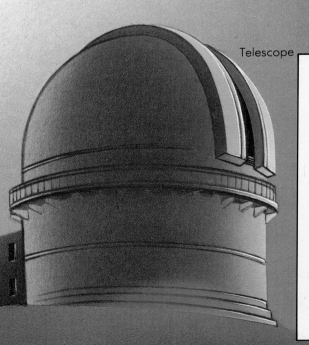

Telescope

MICROSCOPE

It is now possible to see far into the outer reaches of the Universe. It is equally important to look inward at the particles that make up all the matter in space. All matter is made of atoms and even the emptiness of space contains parts of them.

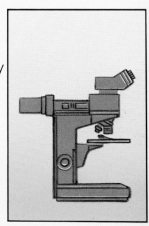

Nebulae

Galaxies

15

The Big Bang

The Universe it is thought, was born in a massive explosion somewhere between 16 and 20 billion years ago, which astronomers call the ''Big Bang.'' It was such a tremendous blast that comparing the Big Bang to an atomic bomb would be like comparing a cap gun to a supernova explosion. Astronomers say that nothing actually existed before the explosion; there was no space or Universe at all, and the Big Bang was the moment when time began.

THE UNIVERSE NOW

After its violent birth, the modern Universe is now filled with clusters of galaxies. As older stars die, their debris reforms as gaseous nebulae, where new stars are born to take their place. The Universe is still expanding; billions of years after the Big Bang, the galaxies are all moving away from each other into space.

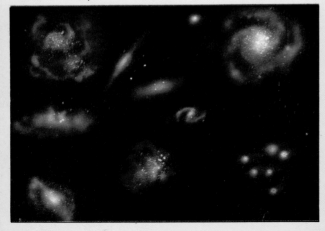

The Infant Universe was a huge spherical fireball which expanded like an inflating bubble. During the first micro-seconds, its temperature was over 100 billion degrees centigrade (°C)! As it expanded it cooled, and when the Universe was three minutes old, its temperature had dropped to "just" one billion degrees. Over the next millions of years, massive clouds of hydrogen began to collect and to collapse in on themselves, forming early galaxies. Later, millions and millions of galaxies formed in massive clusters which make the Universe that exists today.

THE BIG CRUNCH

Can the Universe expand for ever? If the Universe is more dense than now thought, galaxies will expand a certain distance and then start to contract, ending in a Big Crunch (*below*). However, it is currently thought that the Universe will go on expanding indefinitely, with all the galaxies moving steadily away from each other.

The Earth in Space

The Earth is the only planet known to support any sort of life. Water is vital for life to succeed. The Earth is unique in the solar system for having water lying about on the surface. Most other planets are either too hot or too cold and the water either boils or turns to ice. The Earth is 22,000 miles in diameter and the land represents only three-tenths of the surface area. The atmosphere that sustains life is only 30 miles thick, but the dense, or life-supporting part is only 10 miles thick. The Earth is divided into three distinct main layers.

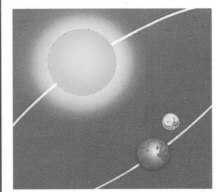

The Earth is one of nine planets orbiting the Sun. It is the third planet from the Sun and orbits at a distance of 93 million miles.

If we travel 200 light years away. (A light year is the distance light travels in one year, about 5.9 trillion miles.) The Sun and all its neighbors have vanished into a star cloud.

Ten thousand light years away, and the Sun and its star cloud become one of dozens of others which together make up one of many spiral arms.

The spiral arm is just one of many which are all joined at their tips to form a galaxy, 100,000 light years across. Our galaxy is called the Milky Way and altogether there are more than 200 billion stars in it.

Inside the Earth

The Earth has three distinct main layers.

The solid layer we live on is the *crust*, divided into the continental region (dry land), and the oceanic region (the ocean floor). This hard, rocky layer, 5 to 25 miles thick, forms 15 slabs or "plates," which fit neatly together and move continuously.

The *mantle* is divided into upper and lower layers. Due to the radioactive decay of its elements, it is a semi-fluid layer which is slowly turned over by convection currents rising from below.

The Earth's *core* is divided into an inner layer and outer layer. The temperature at the center of the core is around 9,000°F, almost as hot as the surface of the Sun. It is made mainly of iron.

To study the structure of the Earth's crust in detail, Soviet scientists are making the world's deepest hole. Drilling in the Kola Peninsula began in 1970, reaching 8 miles in 1987. By 1990, the scientists had reached a depth of over 9 miles (46 times deeper than the Eiffel Tower is high!).

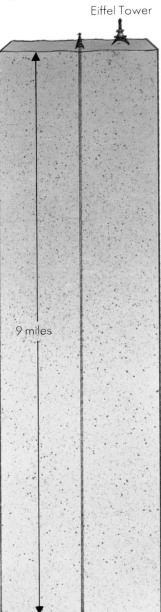

Eiffel Tower

9 miles

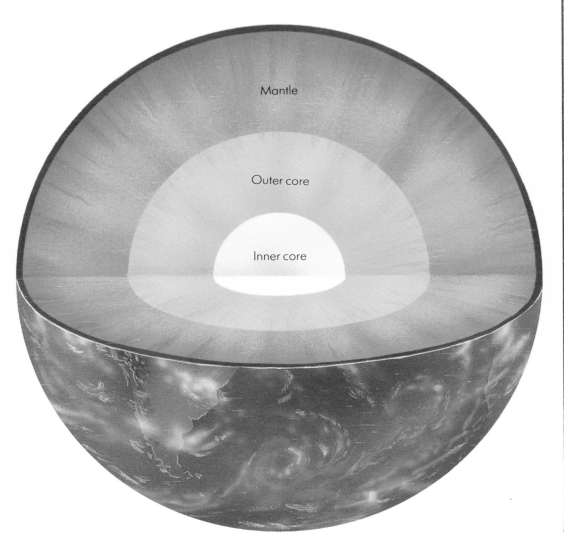

Mantle

Outer core

Inner core

Study of the movement of the 15 different crustal plates is called "plate tectonics." Various things happen where these plates meet:

● When an oceanic plate meets a continental plate, the former is forced down under the latter.
● Where two continental plates collide, mountain ranges such as the Himalayas are forced upward.
● When two plates slide against each other, an unstable earthquake-prone zone is formed, (*below*).

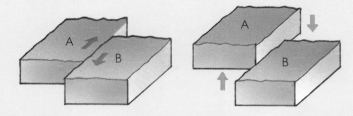

Earthquakes can be so violent that they destroy whole cities. San Francisco, situated on the infamous San Andreas Fault (the boundary between the North American and Pacific plates), was almost destroyed by a huge earthquake in 1906 and suffered damage again in 1989.

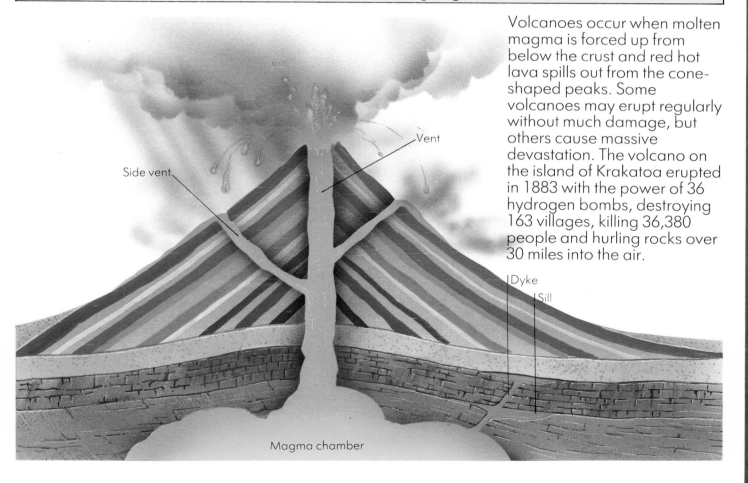

Side vent

Vent

Dyke

Sill

Magma chamber

Volcanoes occur when molten magma is forced up from below the crust and red hot lava spills out from the cone-shaped peaks. Some volcanoes may erupt regularly without much damage, but others cause massive devastation. The volcano on the island of Krakatoa erupted in 1883 with the power of 36 hydrogen bombs, destroying 163 villages, killing 36,380 people and hurling rocks over 30 miles into the air.

The Oceans

More than two-thirds of Earth's surface is covered in water, distinguishing it from all other planets. Earth's oceans not only help to cool the planet, but also have provided humans with fish for thousands of years.

We know less about the undersea world than about the surface of Mars. The ocean floor is a violent, ever-changing place. There are cracks or fractures from which scalding-hot water blasts toward the surface; undersea mountains and volcanoes make Everest seem like a small hill, and deep shadowy trenches descending for thousands of feet, hide creatures we can only imagine . . .

Atlantic

Trench

Mountain ridges

Volcanic island

Pacific

The Earth's oceans are teeming with life, ranging from microscopic plankton to huge whales which move through the oceans like submarines. There are terrifying 10-foot long eels, delicate sea-horses and schools of brightly colored fish among swaying coral. Sadly, we seem determined to exterminate many species through greed, ignorance, and pollution.

POISONING THE SEAS

Sewage and chemicals pumped into the sea return to shore as stinking foam and slime. When oil-laden supertankers rupture, slicks of black oil form over hundreds of miles, killing birds and marine life. Drums of radioactive waste dumped onto the ocean bed will be dangerous for thousands of years to come.

The Moon

The deepest crater on the Moon is "Newton." It is almost 6 miles deep!

The diameter of the Earth is 7,926 miles. The diameter of the Moon is 2,160 miles and its surface area is not much bigger than that of Australia. As it is relatively so large, some astronomers think the Earth and Moon should together be termed a "Double Planet."

It is thought that the Moon was created when, soon after the Earth's formation around 5 billion years ago, an object the size of Mars smashed into it. The collision sent a massive shower of debris into orbit which collided and gradually fused into a large, solid object. Heat from the constant collisions kept the Moon''s surface molten; heavier elements such as iron sank to the center, and the lighter elements floated upward to form a solidifying crust.

The Moon takes exactly the same length of time to make one complete orbit of the Earth as it does to revolve once on its own axis: 27.3 days. This is why we always see the same face of the Moon.

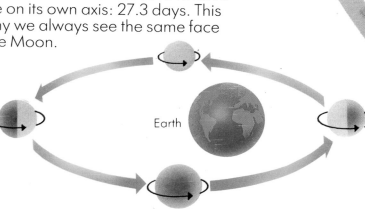

Earth

Moon

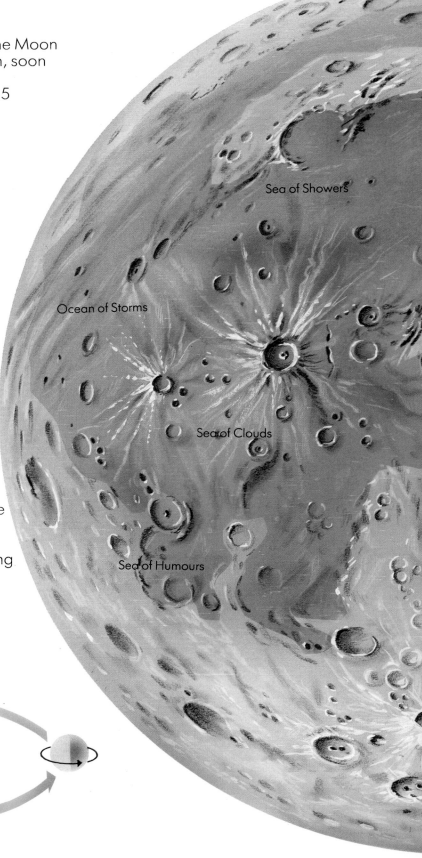

Sea of Showers

Ocean of Storms

Sea of Clouds

Sea of Humours

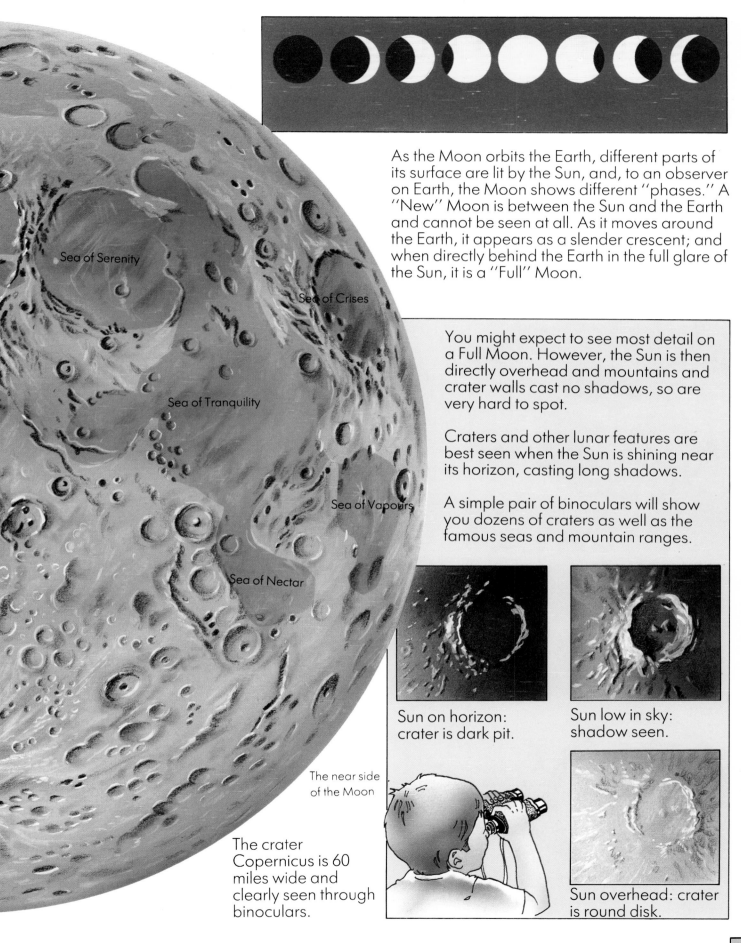

As the Moon orbits the Earth, different parts of its surface are lit by the Sun, and, to an observer on Earth, the Moon shows different "phases." A "New" Moon is between the Sun and the Earth and cannot be seen at all. As it moves around the Earth, it appears as a slender crescent; and when directly behind the Earth in the full glare of the Sun, it is a "Full" Moon.

You might expect to see most detail on a Full Moon. However, the Sun is then directly overhead and mountains and crater walls cast no shadows, so are very hard to spot.

Craters and other lunar features are best seen when the Sun is shining near its horizon, casting long shadows.

A simple pair of binoculars will show you dozens of craters as well as the famous seas and mountain ranges.

Sea of Serenity

Sea of Crises

Sea of Tranquility

Sea of Vapours

Sea of Nectar

The near side of the Moon

The crater Copernicus is 60 miles wide and clearly seen through binoculars.

Sun on horizon: crater is dark pit.

Sun low in sky: shadow seen.

Sun overhead: crater is round disk.

Getting to the Moon

The Soviet Union was the first nation to reach the Moon with its unmanned robot *Luna* probes in 1959. The first probe, Luna 1, sent back information, but no pictures. Ten months later Luna 3 took pictures of the Moon's previously unseen far side. On January 31, 1966 the 9th Luna probe landed on the Moon and returned the first pictures from the surface. Luna probes also gathered small samples of lunar soil and analyzed them.

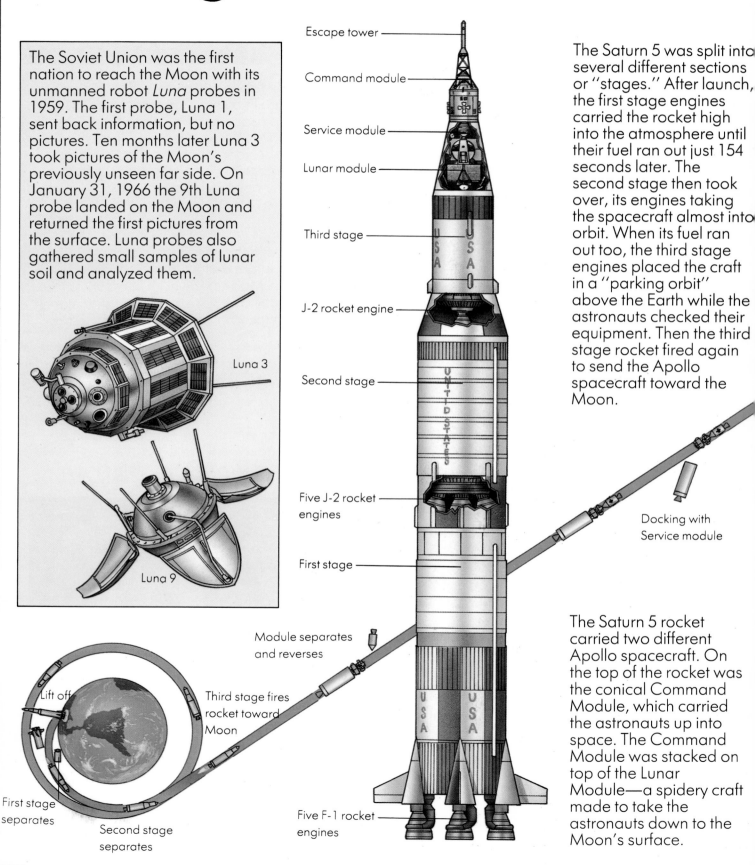

Luna 3

Luna 9

Escape tower

Command module

Service module

Lunar module

Third stage

J-2 rocket engine

Second stage

Five J-2 rocket engines

First stage

Five F-1 rocket engines

Module separates and reverses

Third stage fires rocket toward Moon

Lift off

First stage separates

Second stage separates

Docking with Service module

The Saturn 5 was split into several different sections or "stages." After launch, the first stage engines carried the rocket high into the atmosphere until their fuel ran out just 154 seconds later. The second stage then took over, its engines taking the spacecraft almost into orbit. When its fuel ran out too, the third stage engines placed the craft in a "parking orbit" above the Earth while the astronauts checked their equipment. Then the third stage rocket fired again to send the Apollo spacecraft toward the Moon.

The Saturn 5 rocket carried two different Apollo spacecraft. On the top of the rocket was the conical Command Module, which carried the astronauts up into space. The Command Module was stacked on top of the Lunar Module—a spidery craft made to take the astronauts down to the Moon's surface.

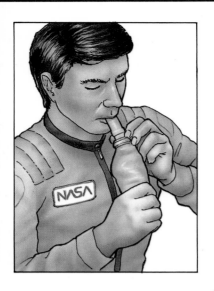

The Apollo astronauts lived in cramped conditions, surrounded by hundreds of instruments and dials. They ate food from small tubes, adding water to make a meal.

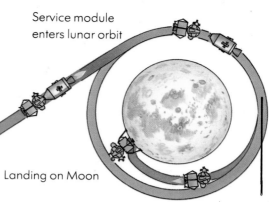

Service module enters lunar orbit

Third stage separates

Landing on Moon

Lunar module separates

The first men to fly to the Moon were the crew of the Apollo 8 mission—Frank Borman, James Lovell, and William Anders. They flew around the Moon in December 1968.

During the flight, the Command Module was joined—or "docked" —to the Lunar Module. Once both the craft were in lunar orbit, two of the crew entered the Lunar Module. The third astronaut remained in the Command Module. The two craft then separated, leaving the Command Module in orbit while the Lunar Module descended to the surface.

The descent was partly controlled by computer, making the engine fire in short bursts to slow the Lunar Module down. Just minutes from the surface, however, the pilot took over, skillfully guiding his spindly craft away from large craters and unexpected fields of boulders.

The Saturn 5 rocket which took men to the Moon stood over 400 feet tall. The gleaming white rocket's mighty engines produced a thrust of over 7,500,000 pounds.

Lunar module

The Surface of the Moon

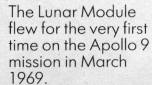

Lunar module

The Lunar Module flew for the very first time on the Apollo 9 mission in March 1969.
One of the astronauts' most important tasks was to bring back samples of lunar rock and soil for analysis and study. They took interesting samples, using special drills to bore below the surface and take long cylindrical rock samples.

The Apollo 11 mission cost over $355 million!

Because of their limited air supply, the astronauts could not spend long away from the Lunar Module. NASA gave the Apollo 15, 16, and 17 crews Lunar Rovers so they could travel farther. These "beach buggies," powered by electric batteries, had a large antenna for communicating with the Earth.

The astronauts also set up various scientific experiments on the Moon, left to continue working after their departure.

Siesmometer

MOONDUST

Commander Neil Armstrong found the Moon surface solid and safe, with a layer of fine, powdery dust which stuck to his boots "like wet sand." There is no air on the Moon to create winds, so the footprints will remain for millions of years.

The Moon is a barren, lifeless world, and without an atmosphere the sky is black and cold. Because it is smaller than Earth the horizon seems very close, and Apollo astronauts reported how they felt the ground curving away below them. The horizon shows rolling hills, and the gray/brown landscape is scattered with boulders and rocks.

On the Apollo 14 mission in 1971, astronaut Alan Shepard used a soil-sample scoop as a golf club and sent a rock shooting across the surface. The Apollo astronauts also enjoyed exercising in the low gravity.

Because no air softens the Sun's light, all shadows on the Moon are a deep black and have sharp edges. The Sun shines brilliantly by day, and the stars by night. The Earth from the Moon resembles a blue marble, frosted over with swirls of white cloud, with phases just like the Moon.

Lunar rover

Return to Earth

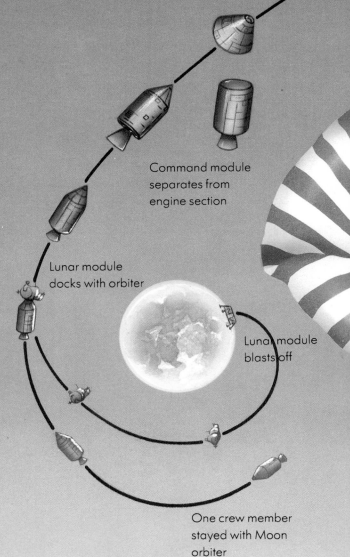

Command module turns around for re-entry – and splashdown

Command module separates from engine section

Lunar module docks with orbiter

Lunar module blasts off

One crew member stayed with Moon orbiter

After completing their tasks, the Apollo astronauts returned to the Lunar Module, fired the engines on the Ascent Stage and took off. They only had one chance for this to work. Had it failed they would have stayed there and died. The Lunar Module docked with the orbiting Command Module, the landing team returned to the Command Module, and the two craft finally separated.

The conical Command Module separated from its engine section in orbit and began to drop down into the atmosphere.

All the early American space missions ended with a "splashdown" in the ocean. When the Command Module hit the water, inflatable cushions kept it afloat until a helicopter came to rescue the astronauts.

As the Command Module dropped through the atmosphere, the friction of air molecules rubbing against its base created heat. Had the base not been covered with a special heat shield, it would have burned up like a meteor.

MOONROCK

The Moon rocks, collected from different sites gave scientists a lot of information. They contained very little oxygen or potassium, but did contain common elements such as calcium, titanium, and aluminum. Tests on tiny fragments of green Moon rock revealed an age of roughly 4.6 billion years. The youngest rock sample was returned by the crew of Apollo 15; it was "just" 3.1 billion years old.

The Solar System

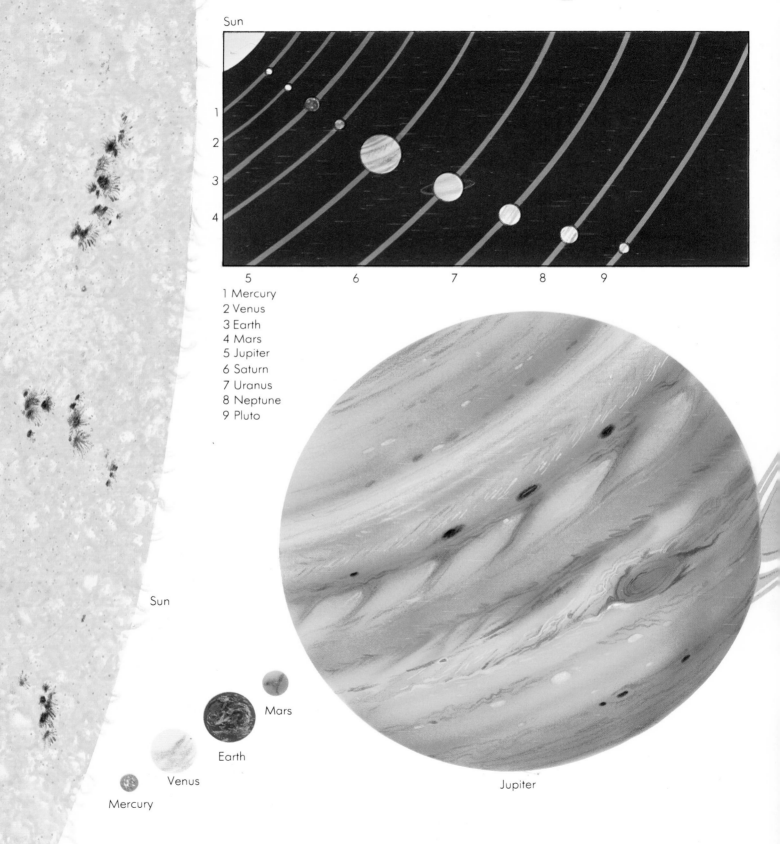

Sun

1
2
3
4

5   6   7   8   9

1 Mercury
2 Venus
3 Earth
4 Mars
5 Jupiter
6 Saturn
7 Uranus
8 Neptune
9 Pluto

Sun

Mercury

Venus

Earth

Mars

Jupiter

Pluto

Neptune

Uranus

Saturn

NOTES: "Length of Day" is equivalent to time taken to make one complete rotation.

MERCURY

Diameter	— 3,000 miles
Size compared to Earth	— 0.4×
Length of Year	— 88 days
Length of Day	— 58 days 16 hours
Distance from SUN	— 36 million miles

VENUS

Diameter	— 7,520 miles
Size compared to Earth	— 0.95×
Length of Year	— 224.7 days
Length of Day	— 243 days (Retrograde)
Distance from SUN	— 67 million miles

EARTH

Diameter	— 7,926 miles
Size compared to Earth	— 1×
Length of Year	— 365.25 days
Length of Day	— 23h 56m
Distance from SUN	— 91 million miles

MARS

Diameter	— 4,200 miles
Size compared to Earth	— 0.5×
Length of Year	— 687 days
Length of Day	— 24h 37m
Distance from SUN	— 142 million miles

JUPITER

Diameter	— 88,780 miles
Size compared to Earth	— 11×
Length of Year	— 11.84 years
Length of Day	— 9h 50m
Distance from SUN	— 484 million miles

SATURN

Diameter	— 74,600 miles
Size compared to Earth	— 9×
Length of Year	— 29.46 years
Length of Day	— 10h 14m
Distance from SUN	— 885 million miles
Distance from EARTH	— 763 million miles

URANUS

Diameter	— 32,188 miles
Size compared to Earth	— 4×
Length of Year	— 84 years
Length of Day	— 20h +/− 3 hours (Retrograde)
Distance from SUN	— 1,783 million miles

NEPTUNE

Diameter	— 30,200 miles
Size compared to Earth	— 3.8×
Length of Year	— 164.8 days
Length of Day	— 21h +/− 2 hours
Distance from SUN	— 2,788 million miles

PLUTO

Diameter	— 1,864 miles
Size compared to Earth	— 0.18×
Length of Year	— 248 years
Length of Day	— 6d 9h
Distance from SUN	— 3,660 million miles

The Sun

The Sun is our very own star and is about 93 million miles away. Light takes eight minutes to reach us from the Sun.

A pinhead of the Sun's core material could kill a person 100 miles away.

Each second the Sun loses some 4.5 million tons of material—that means that every 42 million years, it has lost enough material to make the Earth.

Prominence

Earth

Solar prominences are massive eruptions of flame which leap out from the Sun away into space. They reach an average height of between 20 and 56,000 miles and race away from the Sun at over 2.5 million mph.

Sun

Most sunspots are fairly small, but occasionally a massive group will appear without warning. In 1947 a sunspot was seen with an area that astronomers measured as over six billion square miles.

Sunspots are not really spots at all, but holes in the surface of the Sun. They look dark because they are cooler than the surrounding material.

Sunspot

The surface temperature of the Sun is 10,000°F. At its core, the temperature is 27 million°F.

The Sun has several layers, but is made entirely out of super-hot gases. It is over 109 times bigger than planet Earth.

A Solar prominence sends millions of tons of solar material hurtling out into space—enough to incinerate the Earth.

A solar flare is a burst of deadly radiation. When its energy reaches Earth, it can disrupt radio and TV signals, and causes the Northern Lights.

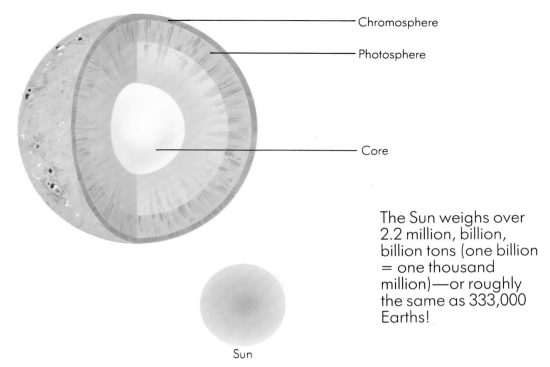

Chromosphere

Photosphere

Core

Sun

The Sun weighs over 2.2 million, billion, billion tons (one billion = one thousand million)—or roughly the same as 333,000 Earths!

SOLAR ECLIPSES

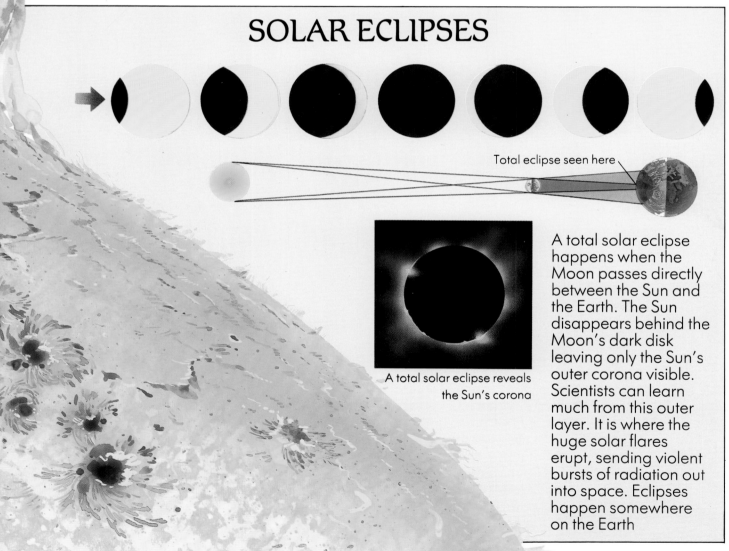

Total eclipse seen here

A total solar eclipse reveals the Sun's corona

A total solar eclipse happens when the Moon passes directly between the Sun and the Earth. The Sun disappears behind the Moon's dark disk leaving only the Sun's outer corona visible. Scientists can learn much from this outer layer. It is where the huge solar flares erupt, sending violent bursts of radiation out into space. Eclipses happen somewhere on the Earth

Mercury

Mercury is a small world; its equatorial diameter of 3,000 miles is roughly one quarter of Earth's and smaller than Jupiter's moon Ganymede!

From Earth Mercury appears as a bright "star" visible for only a short time, either just before sunrise or after sunset. It is very hard to see because it is close to the Sun and is easily lost in the solar glare. It usually appears flashing close to the horizon.

Mariner 10 was 18 inches high, and a little over 4 feet wide. It carried instruments to measure the intensity of magnetic energy, and telescopes which could "see" ultraviolet .radiation. The Mariner 10 probe had also journeyed to Venus, but its most exciting discovery was the cratered, inhospitable world of Mercury. It took over 8,000 photographs.

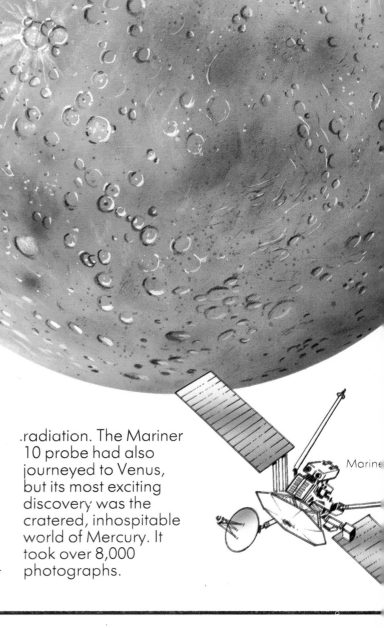

Mercu

Marine

Because Mercury is much closer to the Sun than Earth, the Sun in Mercury's sky appears over twice the size that we see it.

From a distance it looks like our own Moon and is a dark gray, lifeless ball of rock, covered in craters and mountains. As on the Moon, the youngest craters have streaks of bright material spreading out.

Caloris Basin is the largest feature on the surface of Mercury, with a diameter of 800 miles. It was formed when an object 60 miles wide smashed into the planet at a speed of 320,000 mph many millions of years ago. Molten material flooded out over the shattered surface, forming concentric rings. The basin now looks like a bulls-eye target.

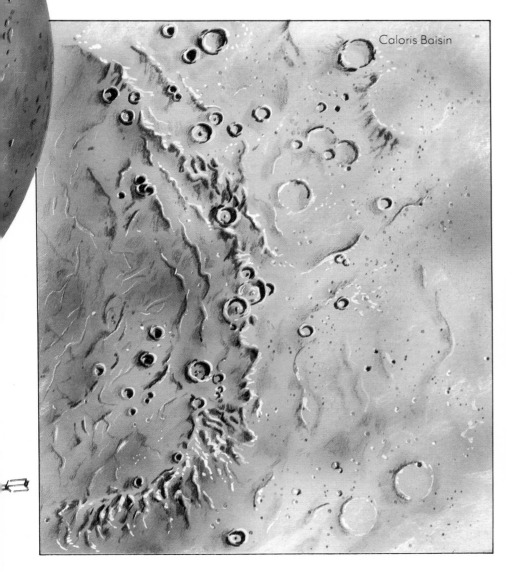

Caloris Baisin

Formation of Caloris Baisin

Venus

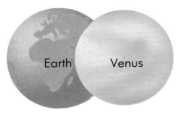

Earth   Venus

Venus has an equatorial diameter of 7,500 miles, just 400 miles smaller than Earth.

Venus, named after the Roman Goddess of love, resembles a brilliant blue-white star. It is only visible for about an hour before sunrise or after sunset, as the planet orbits so close to the Sun.

Earth

Venus

The first probe to transmit data from the surface of Venus was the Soviet Venera 7 probe. In December of 1970 it survived for 23 minutes.

Venus's dense atmosphere means that we cannot see its actual surface directly. Between 1978 and 1980 the American Pioneer-Venus space probe mapped nearly 98% of the planet's surface using radar.

Venus resembles a huge ball of yellow gray smoke without surface features. It has a dense, opaque atmosphere of carbon dioxide cloud and gas. Within this atmosphere, all that is visible are vague "Y" shaped features, revolving around the planet. Venus looks strange because it spins from west to east, the opposite direction to Earth; and so on Venus the Sun rises in the west and sets in the east.

MAGELLAN

The Magellan space probe, launched by a Space Shuttle, will map the surface of Venus in much greater detail, showing craters, volcanoes, and mountains invisible until now.

Magellan probe

Venus's orange clouds form a world of molten, shimmering rocks and fierce winds. Its surface temperature is almost 900°F, even hotter than on Mercury, and quite lethal.

The atmosphere is so dense that its surface pressure is the same as Earth's water pressure on an ocean bed. Such intense pressure has pulverized and crushed surface rocks. The sulfurous atmosphere produces lethal sulfuric acid rain!

Mars

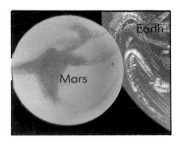

Mars is a small world; its equatorial diameter of 4,217 miles—roughly half the size of Earth. However, because Mars has no oceans, it has the same land area as our own planet.

Early observations of Mars with telescopes showed just a few dark markings on its orange globe—partly because the early telescopes were of poor quality, and partly the planet's atmosphere obscures interesting surface details. More advanced telescopes showed details such as polar caps. Astronomers—especially Percival Lowell—claimed to see dozens of straight lines on the surface and said these were irrigation canals.

The massive Valles Marineris, or "Mariner Valley" was discovered by the Mariner 9 space probe in 1971–72.

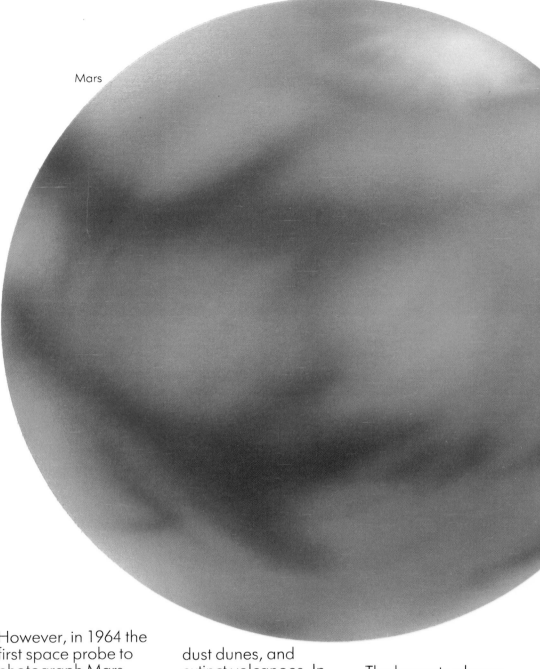

Mars

However, in 1964 the first space probe to photograph Mars successfully, Mariner 4, proved the canals did not exist. Mars was revealed as a dead, desolate world of craters, valleys,

dust dunes, and extinct volcanoes. In color photographs from later probes, it looks like a scarred, pock-marked orange, with a few wisps of silvery cloud and white polar caps.

The largest volcano on Mars is Olympus Mons, named after Mount Olympus. It rises over 15 miles above the Martian desert, over twice as high as Mt. Everest, and is the largest known volcano in the Solar System.

Phobos

Phobos orbits at just 3,717 miles. It is half the size of our Moon and gives off as much light as Venus at its brightest.

Deimos

Deimos is over 14,000 miles from Mars—and would appear from there to be a very bright star.

Olympus Mons

VIKING LANDERS

Viking 1, launched on August 20, 1975, reached Mars in ten months. Viking 2, launched a month after its sister ship, reached the Red Planet three months after Viking 1. The orbiters took photographs while the landers descended to the surface. Their photographs showed a Martian landscape of stony desert— covered with jagged, broken rocks stretching to the horizon and gently sloping.

Viking probe

Study of a Viking 1 orbiter photograph in 1976 revealed an apparently human face with eyes, nose and mouth, framed by an "Egyptian" head-dress. However, the "face" is really just a mesa, or raised platform of rock, and its carved appearance is only a coincidence.

People had expected Mars to be hot, but Viking found that it was very cold and dry, with an average temperature of −9°F.

Jupiter

Jupiter

Earth

The first space probe to visit Jupiter was Pioneer 10 in December 1974.

Jupiter is the largest planet in the Solar System. Its equatorial diameter is 88,730 miles, over 11 times greater than Earth's!

Jupiter appears in the night sky as a bright blue-white star; through a telescope it looks like a yellow-white disk, its face marked with several horizontal belts of dark cloud. From orbit the planet's bloated, orange-brown disk is streaked with dozens of moving cloud belts of different colors.

If you were to represent the Earth as a penny, Jupiter would be as large as a plate.

The four largest and most important satellites of Jupiter are those discovered by Galileo in 1610 and known as the "Galilean" moons: Ganymede, Io, Callisto, and Europa.

Our Moon

Ganymede

Callisto

Voyager 1 revealed a faint, very thin and totally unexpected ring around the planet. This had never been seen from Earth because it was so faint compared to the brilliance of the planet. The whole ring system is approximately 3,679 miles wide, and just over half a mile thick.

ring

The layers of the atmosphere

Water and ice crystals

Ammonium hydrosulphide and ammonia crystals

gaseous hydrogen!

Jupiter has no solid surface on which astronauts could land. Astronomers call it a "Gas Giant," made entirely from different forms of gas.

The surface we see from orbit is merely the planet's highest atmosphere layer. Hidden beneath the shifting clouds of hydrogen, helium, methane, and ammonia is a huge ocean, and beneath that a dense core approximately the size of Earth.

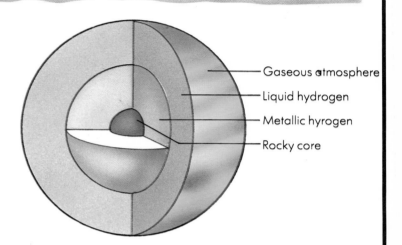

- Gaseous atmosphere
- Liquid hydrogen
- Metallic hyrogen
- Rocky core

Europa

Io

The great red spot

THE RED SPOT

The most dramatic feature on Jupiter, the Great Red Spot, has been observed by astronomers for hundreds of years. Only when the

Voyager space probes explored Jupiter did we fully understood that it is a massive revolving storm over three times the size of Earth!

Saturn

Saturn is the second largest planet in our Solar System with an equatorial diameter of 74,600 miles. It is more than nine times bigger than Earth!

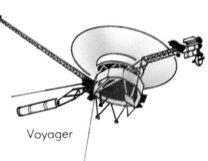

Voyager

Beneath the atmosphere, an ocean of molecular liquid hydrogen enfolds a shell of metallic hydrogen. The center is a rocky core the same size as Earth.

Just like Jupiter, Saturn has a family of orbiting satellites, mostly made of ice. Saturn probably has nearly 24 satellites which orbit it; four are illustrated here. The closest of these moons to Saturn is Mimas, a ball of ice just 240 miles wide orbiting the planet at a distance of 115,330 miles.

Saturn

Dione— orbits 234,574 miles from Saturn and is 696 miles wide, or one third the width of our Moon.

Tethys has a diameter of just over 620 miles and orbits its parent planet at a distance of 183,123 miles.

The next moon is Enceladus. Enceladus is just 68 miles wider than Mimas, and orbits at a distance of 147,890 miles.

Our Moon

Dione

With a large telescope, you can see Saturn's rings clearly, and also the vague markings on its surface.

Tethys

Like Jupiter, Saturn is a "Gas Giant," and its disk is noticeably flattened at the poles to resemble a squashed tennis ball. This is because the planet spins so fast that centrifugal force makes the equator bulge outward.

From Earth only six of Saturn's rings can be seen. Voyager found the rings to be made from many thousands, if not millions, of very thin rings.

Because Saturn's orbit is tipped over slightly compared to Earth's, we occasionally pass through the plane of its rings, either dropping below or rising above the line of the rings. Over a period of time we see

Saturn's rings grow bigger and bigger until wide open (A–C). Then they appear to grow thinner and finally vanish altogether (D–E). The cycle then repeats itself (F–I). The whole process takes about 14 years.

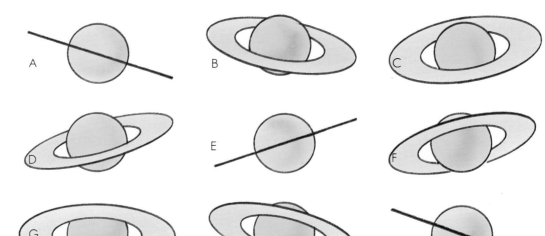

Mimas

Enceladus

SATURN'S RINGS

Saturn's rings are not solid, but more like a blizzard in orbit around the planet's equator. They are made up of particles of rock and ice of different sizes. There are countless thousands of rings made from billions of ring particles, each orbiting the planet like a miniature moon. The impressive rings are very insubstantial, possibly only half a mile thick.

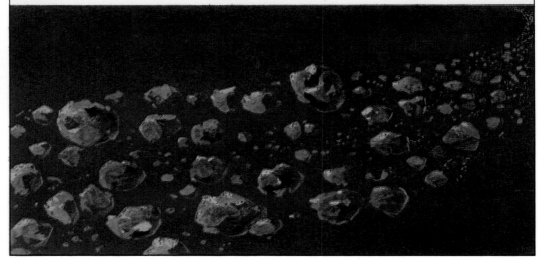

Uranus

Uranus is also tipped over, so that instead of spinning on its poles, it rolls around the Sun on its side like a barrel.

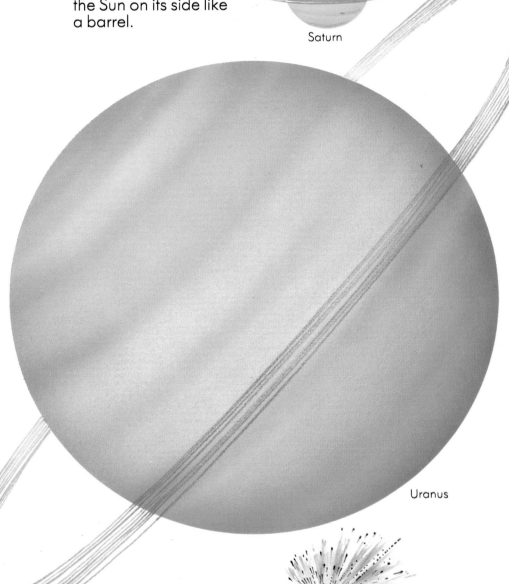

Saturn

Uranus

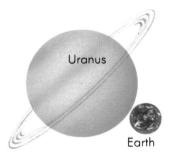

Earth

Uranus lies 1,783 million miles from the Sun. It's diameter is 32,188 miles—four times that of Earth, but only half that of Saturn.

Uranus is so far away that it appears only faintly in the night sky. A telescope shows a tiny blurred green disk, with very vague surface markings.

The Voyager 2 has shown Uranus to be green, because its atmosphere—(mostly hydrogen and helium)—contains methane gas. Methane absorbs red light, so all the light rebounding off the planet becomes a green-blue color. Voyager 2 discovered that Uranus's atmosphere is hidden beneath a deep blanket of haze, like Saturn's moon Titan. The only atmospheric features it found were a few cloud belts and some fast-moving, high altitude streaks of cloud.

It is now thought that Uranus used to orbit in an upright position, until a large comet moving toward the Sun collided with it. The comet smashed into the core with just enough power to knock it over on to its side like a gigantic gyroscope. All Uranus's moons rearranged themselves to orbit around the equator, traveling over and under the planet instead of around its equator.

THE MOONS OF URANUS

Ariel

Umbriel

Titania

Ariel, is almost two and a half times larger than Miranda. It is a very dark world, with deep gouge-like trenches.

Umbriel, virtually the same size as Ariel, has a charcoal-gray surface pitted with craters, some very recent.

Titania is the largest of the major moons, with a diameter of 988 miles. It is almost half the size of our own Moon.

Miranda is a strange, lumpy-looking world, with a mottled, cratered surface, and strange dark "continents" of grooved terrain. But the most fascinating features on Miranda are the ice cliffs, which could be as much as 12 miles high!

Uranus was the first planet discovered by astronomers. All the nearer planets were visible to the naked eye. Uranus was discovered by William Herschel on March 13, 1781, while observing the constellation Gemini.

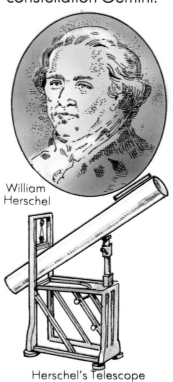

William Herschel

Herschel's Telescope

On March 10, 1977, a team of astronomers were preparing to observe the passage of a star behind the disk of the planet Uranus (an occultation). Half an hour before the occultation was due to begin, the star "winked" unexpectedly and afterwards the star winked again on the *opposite* side of the planet. The astronomers calculated that these objects were a system of rings encircling the planet, like Saturn's.

Uranus's rings

Neptune

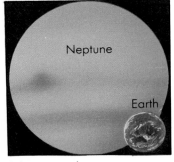

Neptune

Earth

Neptune has an equatorial diameter of 30,200 miles, four times larger than the Earth. Voyager 2's cameras revealed a dynamic and stunningly beautiful planet. It was powder-blue in color, because the methane in its atmosphere absorbs red light, with a huge oval hurricane system, like Jupiter. It also had streamers of bright white cloud, several smaller storm systems, and a broad band of cloud around its south pole.

Neptune

Triton is Neptune's largest moon, just 1,690 miles wide—smaller even than our own Moon! It is an icy world of frozen methane and nitrogen, which has turned pink with exposure to sunlight. Its fascinating surface of craters, valleys, ridges, and frozen methane lakes may also contain erupting volcanoes.

Triton

Voyager made many fascinating discoveries at Neptune, changing astronomers' views of the planet for ever. We now think Neptune's atmosphere covers an "ocean" of liquid methane and ice slush, surrounding in turn a rocky core.

The Scooter, a wedge of blue-white cloud, races around the planet on a "track" half way between its Great Dark Spot and the south pole.

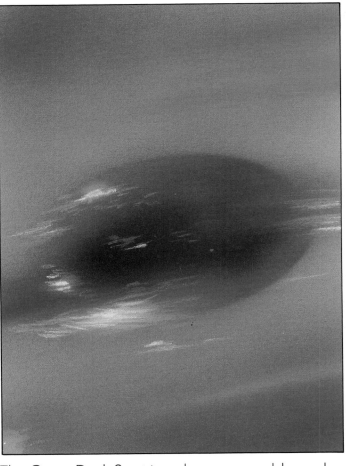

The Great Dark Spot is a deeper gray-blue color than surrounding cloud, and is bigger than the Earth. Like Jupiter's famous Great Red Spot, it appears to be a huge rotating storm system. Voyager's cameras saw streaks of bright "cirrus" cloud above the Great Dark Spot.

Voyager detected shimmering curtains of light "aurorae" on Neptune. Like the aurorae seen on Earth (the "Northern Lights") and Jupiter, they are caused by particles from the Sun interacting with the planet's magnetic field.

Voyager 2 discovered six new moons in orbit around Neptune. They are very small, with diameters less than 300 miles, and resemble the tiny icy satellites of Saturn and Uranus. Photographs taken through Voyager's cameras showed craters on their cold, dark surfaces.

It was believed that Neptune had several partial rings or "ring-arcs" going around it, not a complete ring system. Voyager 2 discovered the arcs were in fact *three* complete rings. The outermost two are the brightest (still much darker than coal) but very narrow, while the inner ring is broader, but very faint. The outermost ring has three strange "clumps" of material spread along it, which astronomers probably mistook for ring-arcs.

Pluto and Planet X

Pluto is a tiny, cold, world 3,660,000,000 miles miles from the Sun. It is 1,864 miles across; just one-tenth the size of Earth, or half the size of Mercury.

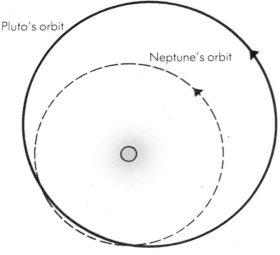

Pluto's orbit

Neptune's orbit

At its most distant point Pluto is over 4,583 million miles from the Sun, but at its closest it is 2,750 million miles away. Thus for a short period it is actually *inside* the orbit of Neptune.

Uranus and Neptune do not orbit the Sun quite as expected and since 1846 Pluto's existence had been suspected. It was discovered almost accidentally by the American astronomer Clyde Tombaugh in February 1930. While photographing the constellation Gemini, he noticed that a small object had moved position (arrow). It had to be a planet. Pluto was named after the King of the Underworld.

Pluto's moon Charon is 740 miles in diameter; so large that they could be called a "double planet." Charon takes 6.4 days to orbit Pluto once.

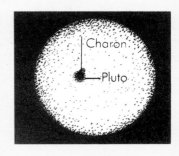

Charon
Pluto

Pluto's surface is probably made from frozen methane. The landscape is hidden beneath atmospheric haze, but would be dominated by eerie ice structures. The Sun would be a bright star in the black sky.

THE SEARCH FOR PLANET X

Planet X may have a highly inclined orbit. This orbit could take it above and below the Sun, rather than moving in the same plane as the other nine planets. The Pioneer and Voyager spacecraft, which have left the Solar System, may give clues about the location of Planet X.

If Planet X exists, it will be very faint and extremely hard to spot among the stars of the Milky Way. Some people believe it lies in the constellation of Scorpius.

Possible orbit of Planet X

Discovery of Pluto's moon Charon proved that Pluto did not cause the eccentric orbits of Neptune and Uranus. Since then a search has been underway for what is responsible. It could be a planet, a black hole, or a huge comet moving slowly in the outermost reaches of the Solar System.

The Stars

Stars, like our Sun, are huge balls of flaming gas fueled by nuclear fusion. Some stars are bigger than the Sun, some smaller, and of different colors and temperatures.

Capella

Capella belongs to the same class as the Sun (Class G), but is larger and 150 times more luminous.

Betelgeuse lies in Orion and is very bright. It is a vivid red M2 star or a red supergiant and swells and shrinks like the human heart. Rigel near Betelgeuse is a brilliant blue-white class B8 star, roughly 50 times bigger than the Sun.

Betelgeuse

Sun

The Sun is a Class G star.

Arcturus is a type K2 star and is orange. It is one of the brightest stars in the sky.

Vega

Vega is a blue color and 55 times brighter than the Sun. It is in Lyra (the Lyre) and is a Class A star.

Arcturus

Sirius, the "Dog Star," is the brightest star in the night sky. It lies near Orion and is 23 times more luminous than the Sun.

Sirius

VV Cephei is a huge variable star and is bluish-white.

VV Cephei

Aldebaran

Aldebaran is a red giant with a diameter of 38 million miles, 90 times more luminous than the Sun.

CLASSES

A very hot star will shine blue and a cooler one yellow, like the flames of a blowtorch or candle. Stars are put into categories depending on how hot they are, as shown below.

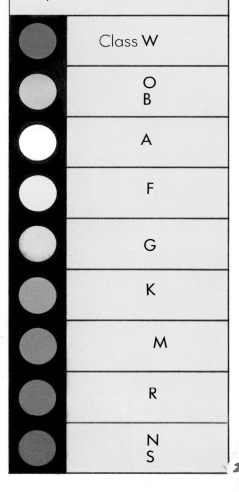

	Class W
	O
	B
	A
	F
	G
	K
	M
	R
	N
	S

The distances of stars are so vast, they are measured in light years (the distance that light can travel in one year, i.e., 5.88 trillion miles). Alpha Centauri, the nearest star to the Sun, is 4.3 light years away.

Many of the stars in the sky are arranged in constellations. They all seem to be the same distance away, but in fact the stars that make up constellations such as the Big Dipper are scattered about in space. The diagram on the right shows the relative distances of the stars in the Big Dipper from the Earth.

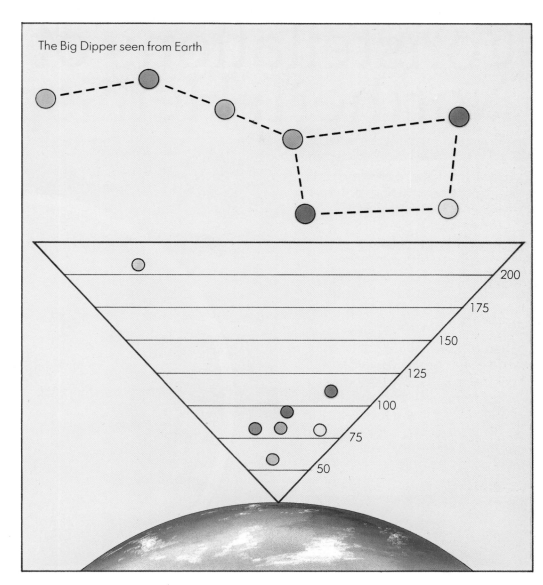

The Big Dipper seen from Earth

MAGNITUDE

It is difficult to tell whether a star is bright because it is huge or because it is near to the Earth. To avoid this problem stars are given an *absolute magnitude*, i.e., how bright they would be if they were *all* 32.6 light years away. For example star B (*below*) seems brighter than A from Earth, but is really much smaller and fainter than A.

From Earth star B looks brighter than A because it is nearer. It is in fact smaller and less luminous.

Sun

B

A

A

B

Constellations of the Northern Hemisphere

The starry sphere of the night sky forms two distinct halves or "celestial hemispheres," divided by the celestial equator. Each celestial hemisphere has interesting features, such as nebulae, star clusters, and constellations, which have been mapped over hundreds of years.

Ursa Major, The Great Bear, is one of the best known of the 88 constellations, and contains the most famous—the Big Dipper, which looks like a large spoon or ladle. The Big Dipper is part of the Ursa Major constellation; its curved handle forms the bear's tail.

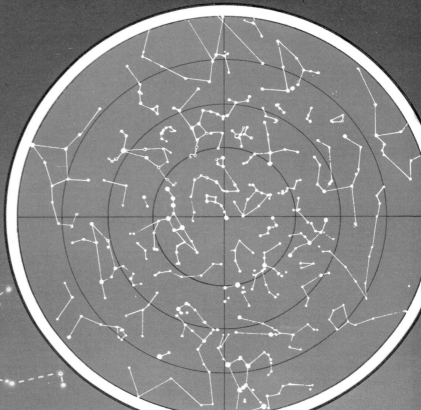

The stars of the Northern Hemisphere

Ursa Major

The stars of the northern hemisphere, with Polaris, the pole star at the center.

Taurus

Canis Major

Orion

The constellation of **Canis Major**, The Great Dog, is the celestial home of Sirius, the "Dog Star," the brightest star in the entire sky. Use Orion's belt of three blue stars to find Sirius; a line extended from the left of the belt toward the horizon points to Sirius.

Taurus The Bull is a large winter constellation built around a "V" of stars on its left side. Ruby red Aldebaran, the brightest star of the "Hyades" cluster, is not a genuine member, but merely lies along that line of vision.

Gemini

Gemini, the constellation of the Heavenly Twins, is dominated by two very bright stars, named Castor and Pollux. A tiny smudge of light near the constellation's base is a star cluster known as M35.

The most dramatic constellation in the northern winter sky is **Orion**, The Hunter. Orion is shaped like a man, with a belt of stars, sword, and raised arm holding a club. The bright red star Betelgeuse is in Orion's left shoulder.

Constellations of the Southern Hemisphere

The southern sky is very different from the northern one. It is dominated by the glittering star clouds of the Milky Way, and also contains a wealth of star clusters, nebulae, and bright stars. The southern hemisphere contains many beautiful sights.

The stars of the Southern Hemisphere

Centaurus

The large, important constellation of **Centaurus**, The Centaur, is home to Alpha Centauri—the star nearest to our Solar System. In fact, Alpha Centauri is actually a system of three stars which lies just over four light years away from us. Proxima, the dimmest star, is nearer than the other two.

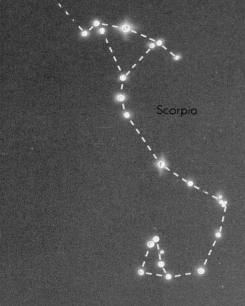

Scorpio

Sagittarius

Magellanic Cloud

Southern Cross

Sagittarius, The Archer, is a medium-sized constellation, shaped rather like an upside down teapot. It lies between us and the core of the Milky Way, apparently embedded in a mass of condensed, glittering star clouds. The brightest stars seem sometimes to vanish in the Milky Way's veil of stars.

The *Small* and *Large* **Magellanic Clouds** (named after the explorer Magellan) are two irregularly shaped galaxies which are satellites of the Milky Way. They are visible to the naked eye as misty clouds of light. The Large Cloud contains the Tarantula Nebula, a cloud of glowing crimson gas, and a supernova which exploded into view in 1987.

The **Milky Way** is best seen from the southern hemisphere, from places such as Australia and South America.

The **Southern Cross** is easily identified, despite its small size and location in the star clouds of the Milky Way. On one side appears to be a dark "hole" in the star fabric of the Milky Way; this is the *Coalsack Nebula*, a vast cloud of dark interstellar gas, silhouetted against the more distant stars of the Milky Way.

Lying to Sagittarius's left is **Scorpius**, the Scorpion, a curved trail of stars, resembling a fish-hook. The constellation is dominated by Antares, a red giant which shines to its left. The trail of stars represents the scorpion's body and wickedly curved tail.

How Stars are Born and Die

Orion Nebula

Matter condenses into protostar

Young stars are bo

The Sun was born five billion years ago. The process of its birth and death is shown here.

A cloud of gas and dust is hit by the shock waves of a distant supernova and begins to condense. As the mass increases, more material is drawn inward and the whole object begins to spin. The material in its center starts to generate heat. When the temperature reaches 18 million °F, nuclear fusion (the making of helium from two hydrogen atoms) begins and the young star is born.

Eventually the Sun will run out of hydrogen and will begin to consume its supply of helium. Burning helium will cause the Sun to swell like an inflating balloon. When the Sun becomes a red giant, it will swallow Mercury and Venus. Heat from the Sun will scorch the Earth's surface.

Finally the star dies

Stars are constantly both being created and dying, but not all suffer the same fate. Stars bigger than the Sun live accelerated lives. Because they are so big, these stars need huge quantities of hydrogen to fuel their nuclear reactions, and so run out of hydrogen very quickly. They eventually blow apart in a huge supernova explosion. Stars smaller than the Sun never become hot enough to light their nuclear fires and slowly fade away.

It cools further

Eventually the star becomes a white dwarf

The star condenses further

The center of the star shrinks and blows off t atmosphere, forming a planetary nebula

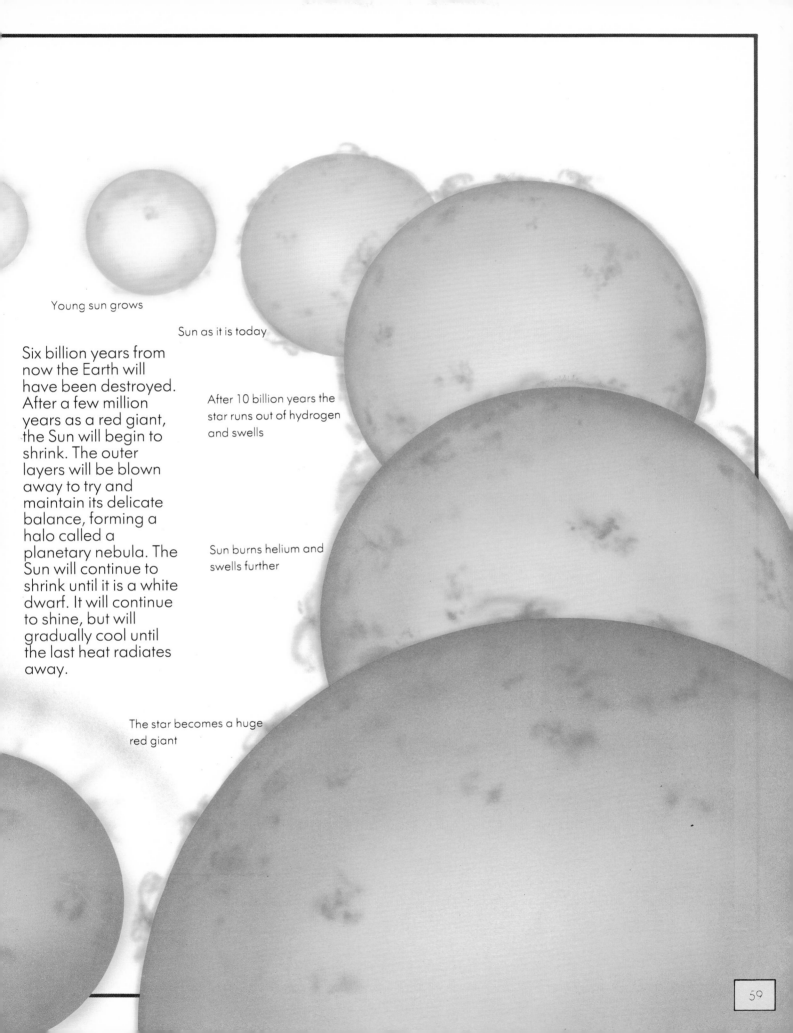

Young sun grows

Sun as it is today

Six billion years from now the Earth will have been destroyed. After a few million years as a red giant, the Sun will begin to shrink. The outer layers will be blown away to try and maintain its delicate balance, forming a halo called a planetary nebula. The Sun will continue to shrink until it is a white dwarf. It will continue to shine, but will gradually cool until the last heat radiates away.

After 10 billion years the star runs out of hydrogen and swells

Sun burns helium and swells further

The star becomes a huge red giant

Supernovae

Star exhausts hydrogen supply

Begins to burn helium

Core shrinks and burns heavier fuel

Core is now made of iron

Iron core explodes

A supernova is the result of the violent death of a massive star. In the first ten seconds of the explosion, it produces 100 times more energy than the Sun during the whole of its 10 billion year lifetime ...!

If the next supernova is exceptionally bright (and we are overdue for a supernova of apparent magnitude −14!)it will cast shadows, and be too painfully bright to study through binoculars or a telescope. As the shifting atmosphere makes it twinkle, it will change color from red to blue, then white and then red again.

After exhausting its supply of hydrogen the star's interior contracts, and its temperature soars. This increase in core temperature ignites a new and heavier fuel—the gas helium. However, the helium is soon burned and a replacement fuel is sought. The core contracts and the increase in temperature ignites an even heavier fuel. Eventually only a dense core of iron remains, surrounded by layers of silicon, oxygen, carbon, helium, and hydrogen. The iron core then separates into two regions; the inner region, which collapses quickly, and the outer core, which collapses much more slowly.

Eventually the inner core rebounds, slamming into the contracting outer core. The shock wave in the interior triggers one nuclear reaction after another. The star is literally split apart, and the core becomes a *neutron* star, so dense that just a teaspoonful weighs hundreds of tons.

Explosion produces supernova. Temperatures can reach 180,000°F.

Expended gas cloud drifts away into space

Core becomes a super-dense Neutron star

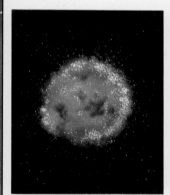

On November 11, 1572, the Danish astronomer Tycho Brahe saw a brilliant new star in the constellation of Cassiopeia. This supernova, was 10,000 light years away. Its absolute magnitude of −16.5 made it more than 300 million times brighter than the Sun.

The brightest supernova for 383 years appeared in February 1987 in the Magellanic cloud in the Southern Hemisphere. It represented the death of a blue giant 20 times bigger than the Sun and 80,000 times as bright, and gave scientists a unique view of the death of a star.

Black Holes and Strange Stars

Gas and material lying close to the black hole are attracted to it like water going down a plug hole. Some astronomers think that the more a black hole "eats," the bigger it becomes. If this is true, there may be Super Black Holes "eating" the equivalent of three Earths every second—or 111 million every year!

If we could travel into space to a black hole, what would it look like? In a region of empty space, it would literally appear as a hole in space. If it was near a cloud of interstellar gas, material drawn toward the star would spiral around it into a disk. It would shine with different types of radiation, giving the dark, central core a glowing halo of light.

Black hole

A black hole is not a "hole," but a solid, spherical object formed after the death of a massive star. After the star has died, all that remains is a tiny, super-dense star several miles wide. Its gravitational pull is so strong that not even light can escape it; so it appears as a black hole cut into the background stars.

Nearby star

In 1962 a small rocket detected strong X-ray radiation in the constellation of Cygnus. Five years later, astronomers located the radiation source as a black hole—possibly the remnant of an ancient star from a supernova explosion. Material is drawn away from nearby stars in a glowing stream then coiled and spiraled around the black hole before it is sucked to oblivion.

Astronomers believe that a massive black hole lies at the center of our Milky Way. Using special instruments they have detected a strong radiation source and radio waves a billion miles in diameter (roughly the distance between Earth and Saturn). At the very center of this object might lie a supermassive black hole, 9 million miles wide!

RED GIANT

When a star the size of our Sun has consumed all its fuel, it briefly swells into a huge red giant, before shrinking to become a white dwarf roughly the size of Earth. A white dwarf is a super dense object, from which a handful of matter would weigh thousands of tons! There are several. The brightest star in the sky, Sirius, has a tiny white dwarf companion, Sirius B, just 12,000 miles wide.

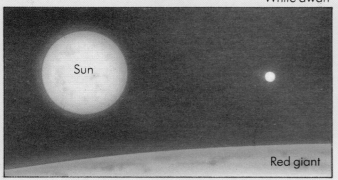

White dwarf

Sun

Red giant

NEUTRON STAR

A neutron star is the core of a star three or more times more massive than the Sun which has been in a supernova explosion. One pinhead of its strange material would weigh more than one million tons—more than the biggest aircraft carrier in the world! Many neutron stars are *pulsars*. Pulsars are rapidly spinning stars that send out beams of radiation that sweep across space.

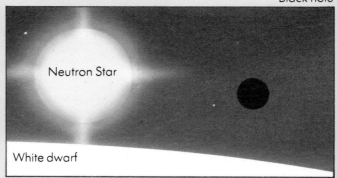

Black hole

Neutron Star

White dwarf

Galaxies

Galaxies are vast collections of stars, gas and dust, held together in one of several different shapes by gravity. They are the "building blocks" of the Universe. Our Milky Way is just one of millions of galaxies drifting through space, and astronomers often call the Milky Way our "island" in the ocean of space. Although our home galaxy is massive when compared to our solar system, it is just one tiny part of the Universe.

Spiral galaxy

Spiral galaxies are shaped like pinwheels, with several spiral arms curving away from their center. Some spiral arms are wound much more tightly than others, and contain not only stars, but also dark trailing lanes of dust and clouds of glowing gas. At their center is a bulging nucleus of old red stars, possibly surrounding a massive black hole. Three fourths of all the galaxies in the Universe are Spirals, and our Milky Way is typical of these.

Barred spiral galaxy

Barred spiral galaxies are very similar to Spiral galaxies, but their spiral arms curve away from the opposite ends of a bar, passing through the center of the nucleus. They contain large amounts of gas and dust as well as stars.

Elliptical galaxy

Irregular galaxy

Elliptical galaxies are huge collections of stars with an elliptical or egglike shape. They consist almost entirely of stars and contain very little gas or dust.

Irregular galaxies are, as their name suggests, irregular collections of stars without any definite shape.

NEW GALAXIES

A typical spiral galaxy begins when a massive dust and gas cloud begins to collapse in on itself, into a roughly spherical shape. Condensations form and become star clusters.

The denser, central portions of the sphere flatten out into a revolving disk. After a billion years or so, spiral arms begin to form out of the disk, containing dense lumps of material which contract further

to form clusters of unstable stars. These explode soon after, spewing rich stellar material through the young galaxy to re-condense into smaller, more stable stars—like our own Sun.

The Milky Way

The Milky Way is just one among 100 billion galaxies in the Universe. It contains over 200 billion stars.

The Milky Way is a massive pinwheel of over 100 billion stars. Our sun is just one of these.

Just like a giant pinwheel, our galaxy rotates. To make one complete revolution takes 230 million years—since it was formed, our galaxy has revolved 52 times.

The nucleus of our galaxy is red because it is made up of ancient, red giant stars. Astronomers think a giant black hole lies in the center.

We are here

The milky way from earth

From Earth we can see the Milky Way as a broad band of misty light, at its brightest during summer.

As well as rotating, the Milky Way is actually moving through space at a speed of 1.4 million miles per hour.

Seen from the side, the Milky Way resembles a discus. Our solar system lies two-thirds of the way from the center.

The Solar System

Star Clusters

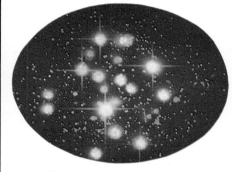

There are many star clusters in our galaxy. Open clusters contain hundreds of stars while denser globular clusters contain millions of stars.

Nebulae are clouds of gas which lie between the stars. They can be either dark or, if they reflect the light of nearby stars, bright.

The Milky Way is constantly producing new stars from all the material within its spiral arms.

Comets

Comets are thought to come from a halo of over 100 billion comets surrounding our Solar System far beyond the orbit of Pluto.

People used to think comets were fireballs, but the exact opposite is true. They are frozen, lifeless bodies most of the time and wake up only when they near the Sun.

A comet's nucleus is like an iceberg. As it nears the Sun, the ice melts, releasing the gas trapped inside.

Some comets pass so close to the Sun that astronomers call them "sun-grazers." In 1965, Comet Ikeya Seki passed just 290,000 miles above the Sun's surface.

A comet's tail always points away from the Sun. The gases released from the nucleus get blown behind it by the solar wind.

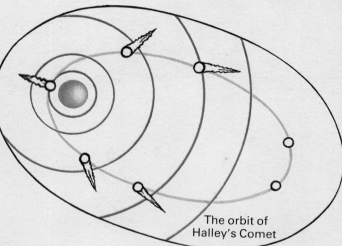

The orbit of Halley's Comet

Most comets appear to have only one tail but some have more. Comet de Cheseaux had six.

The Great Comet of 1843 had the longest recorded tail, stretching over 500 million miles— roughly the same distance as the Earth is from Jupiter.

A comet has two tails. The dust tail is yellow because it reflects sunlight, and the gas tail is blue because it shines with its own light.

HALLEY'S COMET

The most famous comet is Halley's Comet. It can be traced far back into history—William the Conqueror saw it in 1066. It was last seen in 1986, and will return in 2068.

In 1986 the space probe Giotto took close-up photographs of Halley's comet. Seconds later it was knocked off course by a blast of dust.

Meteors and meteorites

Shooting stars which astronomers term "meteors," are not really stars, but much smaller objects. They range in size from a grain of rice to several inches. A meteor plunges into our atmosphere, and becomes very hot because of the air molecules rubbing against it. For a split second it is visible, glowing like a star and shooting across the sky. The dust soon burns to a cinder, and vanishes. Meteors are pieces of material left over from the birth of the Solar System five billion years ago.

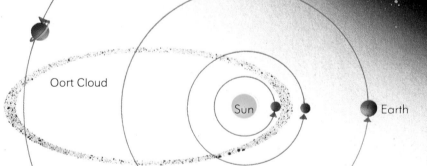

Oort Cloud

Sun

Earth

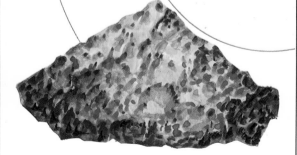

Most shooting stars burn up completely, but one large enough may fall to Earth as a charred piece of rock, or meteorite.

HUNTING METEORITES

Meteorites are difficult to find because they are small and easily lost on the ground. However, Antarctica is excellent for meteorite-hunting, as the charred stones stand out clearly against the snow and ice. Often they are just lying on the surface.

Some are colored, most often blue and white, though some may be red, or even green.

In 1966, a magnificent display of shooting stars occurred, and for a brief period over 1,000 meteors were flashing across the sky every second! Some observers said the shooting stars were "falling like snow." It was called the Leonid Shower.

On any clear night you can expect to see at least one bright shooting star. Some are barely visible, others bright enough to cast shadows. Most are as bright as an average star, and easy to spot.

The best known crater on Earth is the huge "Meteor Crater" in Arizona. It is three-fourths of a mile wide, more than 600 feet deep, and only properly visible from the air. It was formed 50,000 years ago, when a large meteorite 100 feet wide and weighing over 100,000 tons struck the Earth.

Space Travel Origins

By A.D. 970 the Chinese had designed a bamboo tube filled with gunpowder on the tip of a long arrow. When fired, this "rocket-arrow" would travel a long distance over battlefields before exploding.

The world's first ever artificial satellite, Sputnik 1, was launched on the October 4, 1957 by the Soviet Union. Tiny compared to today's massive communications satellites, Sputnik 1 was really a polished metal sphere the size of a beach-ball with a radio transmitter inside.

In April 1961, Major Yuri Gagarin became the first man into space. He traveled around the Earth in Vostok 1, a modified unmanned satellite, for 1 hour and 18 minutes, and returned to Earth 108 minutes after leaving the launch pad.

During World War II German scientists built a rocket to attack London from the continent. Each V2 rocket was 46 feet high, had a range of 200 miles and carried 11,000 pounds of explosives. After the war the V2 scientists helped the United States to develop a space rocket.

The first live creature to f[ly] in space was a fox terrie[r] called Laika. She was carried aboard Sputnik [2] on November 3, 1957, and spent a week in orb[it]. There was no way to bring her back to Earth alive, and she died in he[r] sleep when the capsule'[s] oxygen ran out.

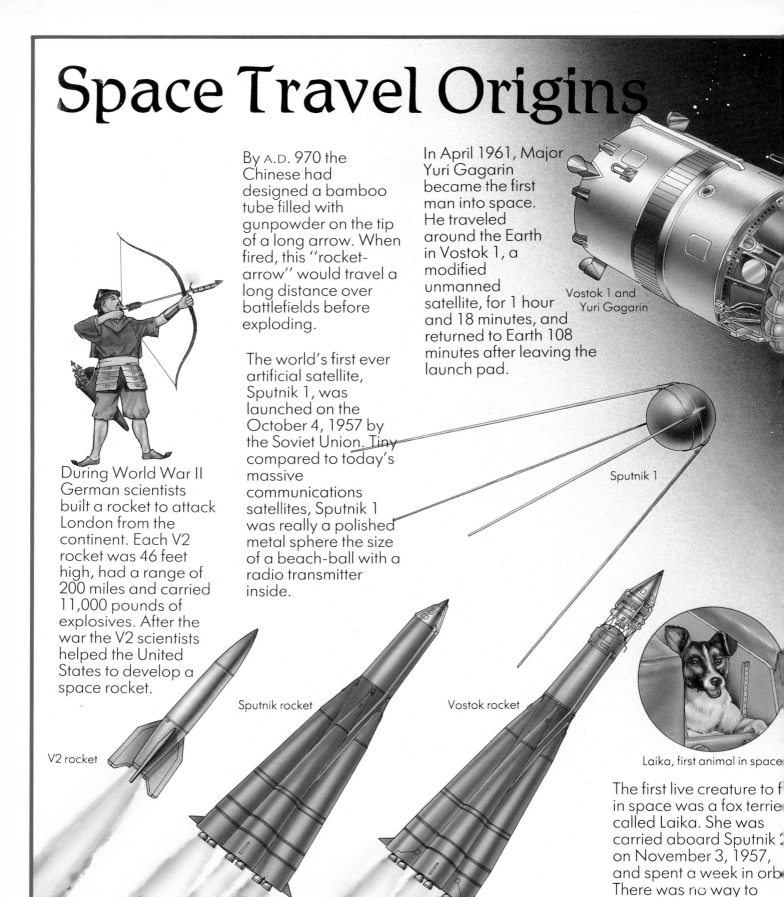

Vostok 1 and Yuri Gagarin

Sputnik 1

Sputnik rocket

Vostok rocket

V2 rocket

Laika, first animal in space

Gemini 7

Skylab

The U.S. Skylab space station was an American triumph. The "workshop" of the station was actually a converted rocket stage which contained experiments, work stations, food stores, and living quarters. Skylab crews traveled to the space station in modified Apollo spacecraft, and docked into a cylindrical docking adapter. Power for Skylab was provided by solar cells mounted on two large wing-like panels, only one of which actually opened.

The Gemini program, costing $1 billion, linked spacecraft in oribit as a first step in sending astronauts to the Moon.

The Space Shuttles

The Shuttle climbs into final orbit using thrusters.

Then the main fuel tank is jettisoned.

The solid rocket boosters are jettisoned.

The shuttle blasts off,

Space shuttles go into space like a rocket, but land like a plane. An orbiter is very like a plane, with a flight deck, wings and tailfin, landing gear and brakes, and a crew of up to eight. The forward part of the craft contains the flight deck, instruments and computers; the lower "mid-deck", contains experiments.

The space shuttle carries satellites, laboratories, and other important cargoes into space inside its huge payload bay, large enough to hold five elephants!

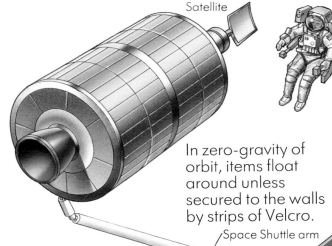

Satellite

In zero-gravity of orbit, items float around unless secured to the walls by strips of Velcro.

Space Shuttle arm

To maneuver payloads in and out of the cargo bay, orbiter uses a long robot arm, controlled by an astronaut on the flight deck with a joystick.

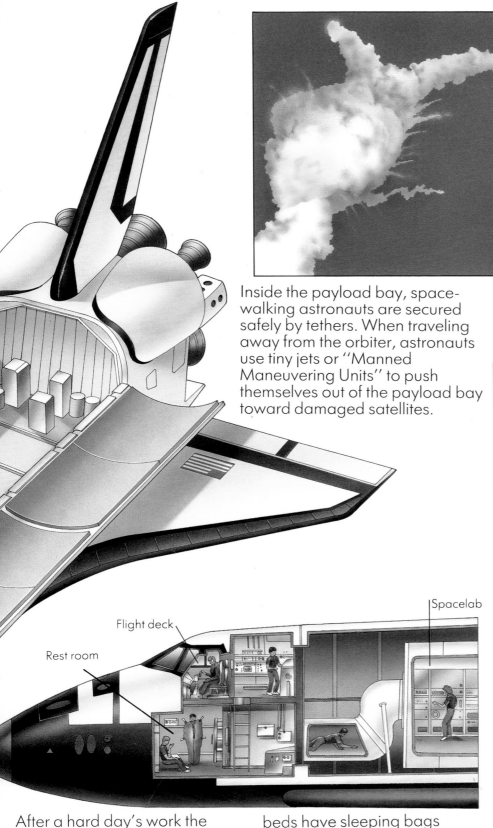

In 1986, the space shuttle Challenger blasted off from the launch pad for the 25th Shuttle mission. On board were six American astronauts and a school-teacher, Christa McAuliffe, the first civilian to fly in space. Seventy three seconds after blast-off, the shuttle exploded and all the astronauts were killed. The disaster happened because one of the solid rocket boosters was faulty.

Inside the payload bay, space-walking astronauts are secured safely by tethers. When traveling away from the orbiter, astronauts use tiny jets or "Manned Maneuvering Units" to push themselves out of the payload bay toward damaged satellites.

Rest room

Flight deck

Spacelab

After a hard day's work the crew retire to their beds. Two of the beds are like chests of drawers, with doors which slide shut; the third bed is vertical, like a shower cubicle. All the beds have sleeping bags instead of mattresses, and straps secure the astronauts to prevent them from drifting around in the weightless conditions.

THE RUSSIAN SHUTTLE

The Soviet Space Shuttle, is called Buran ("Snowstorm") almost exactly like its American counterpart. The difference? Buran has no engines and reaches orbit on the side of a rocket.

Satellites

A communications satellite bounces signals sent from one point on the Earth back down to another point. Among the most important comsats are the Intelsats, which transfer international telephone calls. **Intelsat 5**, the latest satellite in the Intelsat network, run by 100 countries, can carry up to 33,000 simultaneous telephone conversations.

From their orbits, "Earth Resource" satellites such as **Landsat** take thousands of pictures of the Earth's surface, mapping areas of vegetation and mineral deposits. As well as surface geology, the satellite searches underground, to locate water under the desert and potential areas for oil exploration under the ocean. The satellites can also take high resolution photographs of towns and cities.

Meteosat, a weather satellite, orbits in a geostationary orbit, appearing to hover 22,300 miles above the equator. It can take several different types of pictures at once. One camera photographs visible light features like clouds.

Landsat

Intelsat

The KH-11 spy satellites —nicknamed "KEY-HOLE"—can stay in orbit for over two years. More than 60 feet tall and weighing nearly 30,000 pounds, their highly sensitive sensors can zoom in on individual soldiers hundreds of miles below!

Another camera takes infrared shots of different temperature areas. Another camera might measure narrow infrared wavelengths. They also record areas of atmospheric humidity.

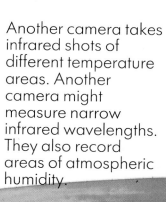

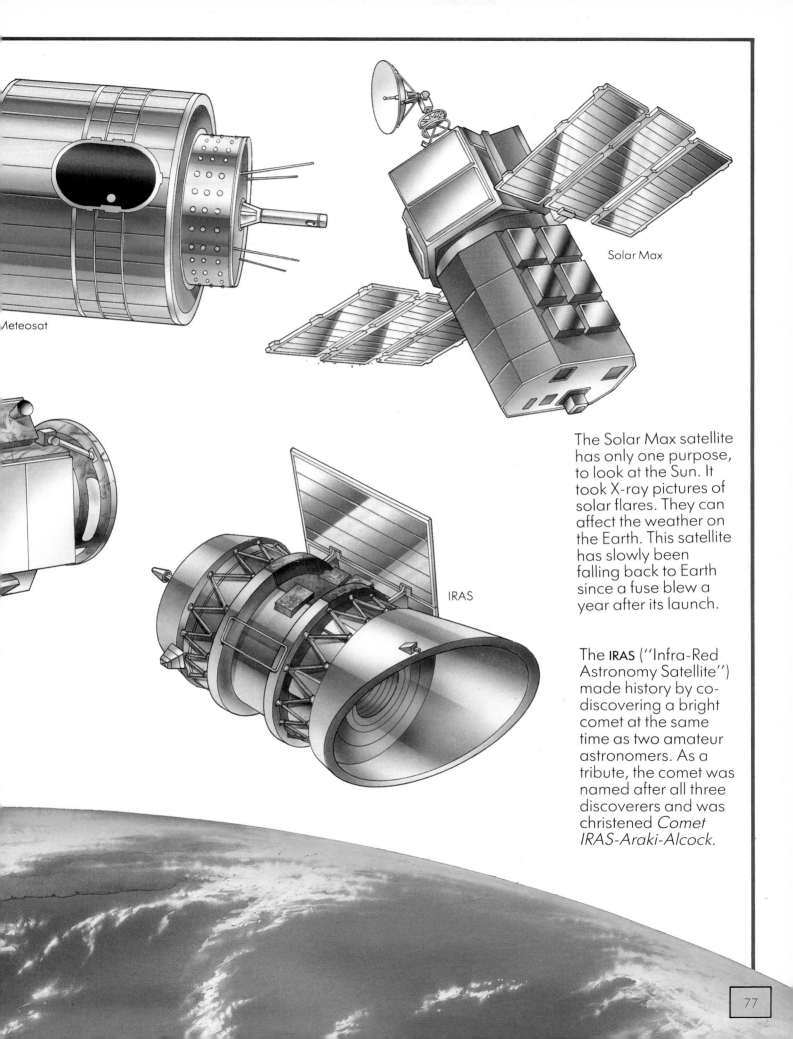

Meteosat

Solar Max

IRAS

The Solar Max satellite has only one purpose, to look at the Sun. It took X-ray pictures of solar flares. They can affect the weather on the Earth. This satellite has slowly been falling back to Earth since a fuse blew a year after its launch.

The IRAS ("Infra-Red Astronomy Satellite") made history by co-discovering a bright comet at the same time as two amateur astronomers. As a tribute, the comet was named after all three discoverers and was christened *Comet IRAS-Araki-Alcock.*

Space Probes Explore the Solar System

During the past 30 years many space probes have been sent to explore the Solar System, and all the planets except Pluto have now been visited. Mariner 10 (1) reached Mercury in March 1974 taking more than 8,000 photographs of the barren, cratered landscape. It is now in permanent orbit around the Sun. The Pioneer Venus orbiter (4) traveled 300 million miles, reached Venus in December 1978, and sent back radar maps of the Venusian surface. Viking probes (3) landed on the surface of Mars in 1975 by parachute, tested the soil for signs of life and found none. Voyagers 1 and 2 explored the outer planets. Voyager 2 (2) sent back stunning pictures of Neptune. Magellan (5) should reach Venus in August 1990 and Galileo (6) will be launched from a shuttle to explore the giant Jupiter.

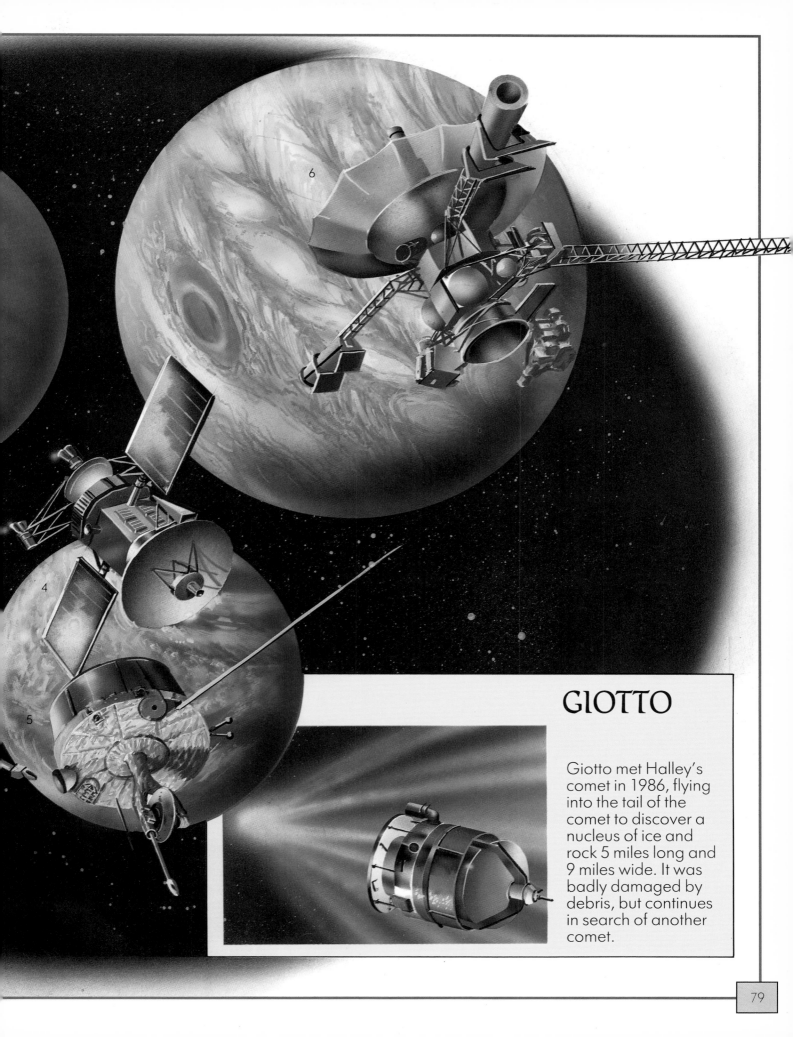

6

4

5

GIOTTO

Giotto met Halley's comet in 1986, flying into the tail of the comet to discover a nucleus of ice and rock 5 miles long and 9 miles wide. It was badly damaged by debris, but continues in search of another comet.

Voyager

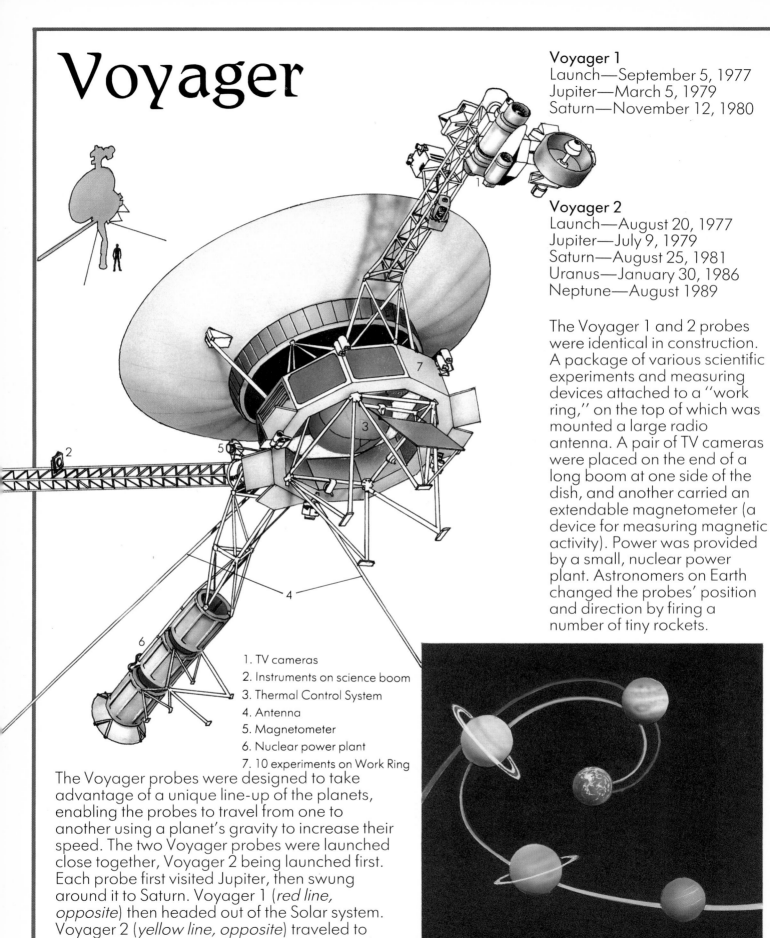

Voyager 1
Launch—September 5, 1977
Jupiter—March 5, 1979
Saturn—November 12, 1980

Voyager 2
Launch—August 20, 1977
Jupiter—July 9, 1979
Saturn—August 25, 1981
Uranus—January 30, 1986
Neptune—August 1989

The Voyager 1 and 2 probes were identical in construction. A package of various scientific experiments and measuring devices attached to a "work ring," on the top of which was mounted a large radio antenna. A pair of TV cameras were placed on the end of a long boom at one side of the dish, and another carried an extendable magnetometer (a device for measuring magnetic activity). Power was provided by a small, nuclear power plant. Astronomers on Earth changed the probes' position and direction by firing a number of tiny rockets.

1. TV cameras
2. Instruments on science boom
3. Thermal Control System
4. Antenna
5. Magnetometer
6. Nuclear power plant
7. 10 experiments on Work Ring

The Voyager probes were designed to take advantage of a unique line-up of the planets, enabling the probes to travel from one to another using a planet's gravity to increase their speed. The two Voyager probes were launched close together, Voyager 2 being launched first. Each probe first visited Jupiter, then swung around it to Saturn. Voyager 1 (*red line, opposite*) then headed out of the Solar system. Voyager 2 (*yellow line, opposite*) traveled to Uranus and Nepture before it also left the Solar System.

VOYAGERS' DISCOVERIES

Jupiter

Saturn

The Voyagers took amazing photographs of Jupiter's swirling, multi-colored clouds.

The Voyager probes discovered Saturn's rings were made of thousands and thousands of tiny ringlets. They discovered many new small moons in orbit and took detailed pictures, of its major moons, including Mimas and Titan.

Io

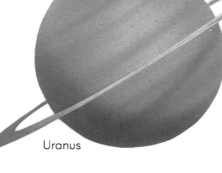

Uranus

Neptune

Voyager 1 discovered active sulfur volcanoes on Jupiter's orange moon Io.

Voyager 2 revealed Uranus to be a bland, featureless world. Its tiny moon, Miranda, was revealed as the most fascinating satellite of the solar system, with towering ice cliffs and a strange, grooved surface.

Neptune was powder-blue, with a storm called the Great Dark Spot. Voyager showed astronomers the moon Triton's surface for the first time.

A MESSAGE

In case any other being found the drifting Voyager, scientists fixed a plaque and a record onto its side. The plaque shows a man, woman, and child, and a simple map to show Earth's location in space. The record contains sounds, ranging from classical music to greetings in many languages. The record could also show them 118 pictures, including a human skeleton, the ocean, a snow-topped mountain and, of course, the Earth seen from space.

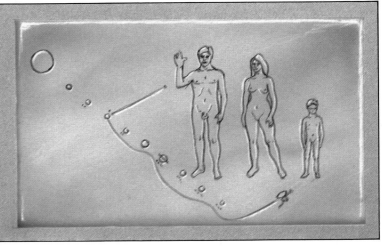

The Attempts to Reach Mars

Many different spaceprobes have visited Mars over the years. Several American MARINER probes were sent to the Red Planet in the 1960s and 1970s and took the first detailed pictures of its surface. They were followed by the more sophisticated VIKING probes which analyzed the soil in mini laboratories.

In 1994 the Soviet Union will explore Mars with several balloons. These will drift around Mars taking photographs and making measurements of wind speeds, etc. These balloons will be followed by Robot Rovers, which will trundle across the plains under remote control. Before a manned expedition is staged a sample of Martian soil will be taken by a robot lander and returned to Earth.

The US hopes to send a manned mission to Mars after they have built the Freedom space station and established a base on the Moon. Astronauts may head for Mars in the year 2011. The Mars spaceship will be so large that it will be built in orbit, assembled from different sections carried into orbit by rockets and space shuttles. It will have powerful rocket motors and several Landers.

While the Landing Team explore the Martian surface, the astronauts left behind in the Mothership will study Mars from orbit.

When the ship enters Martian orbit her crew will finally select the landing site by photographing the surface through high powered telescopes. Then they will check the systems of the Lander craft itself.

After separating from the Mothership the Lander will leave orbit by firing rockets to slow it down. After flying through the atmosphere it will drop to the surface on parachutes, slowed by its braking engines.

After the astronauts from the first Lander have explored their landing site, taking rock samples and setting up instruments, other Landers will descend to the surface, landing nearby to create a Mars Base.

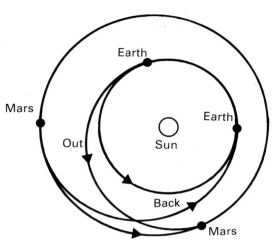

To reach Mars, the astronauts will have to spend three years in space. If they set off for Mars in December 1999 they would reach their destination 9 months later. After spending four months on the surface they would set course for Earth once more, returning home in September 2001.

After docking with the Mothership the triumphant explorers will rejoin their crewmates and prepare for the return to Earth. They will take final photographs of Mars and dump all their waste into space before shutting down all the Mothership's systems and entering the Return stage, carrying with them all the photographs, rock samples, and data they have gathered during their stay. The crew will fire the Return stage's engines and leave Mars orbit for Earth, leaving the Mothership behind as a Mars Orbital Space Station.

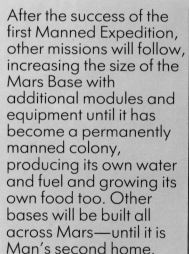

After securing their Base against the elements and shutting down all its power systems the astronauts will strap themselves into the upper stage of a Lander. Using the descent stage as a launch pad the Upper Stage will blast-off and head for an orbital rendezvous with the Mothership.

After the success of the first Manned Expedition, other missions will follow, increasing the size of the Mars Base with additional modules and equipment until it has become a permanently manned colony, producing its own water and fuel and growing its own food too. Other bases will be built all across Mars—until it is Man's second home.

Man in Space

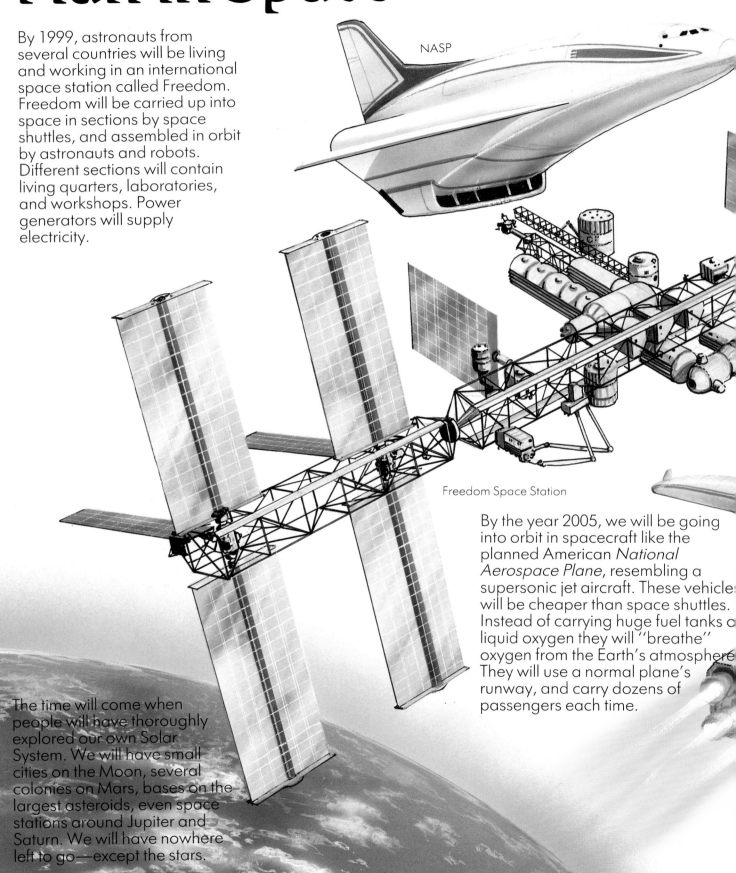

By 1999, astronauts from several countries will be living and working in an international space station called Freedom. Freedom will be carried up into space in sections by space shuttles, and assembled in orbit by astronauts and robots. Different sections will contain living quarters, laboratories, and workshops. Power generators will supply electricity.

NASP

Freedom Space Station

By the year 2005, we will be going into orbit in spacecraft like the planned American *National Aerospace Plane*, resembling a supersonic jet aircraft. These vehicles will be cheaper than space shuttles. Instead of carrying huge fuel tanks of liquid oxygen they will "breathe" oxygen from the Earth's atmosphere. They will use a normal plane's runway, and carry dozens of passengers each time.

The time will come when people will have thoroughly explored our own Solar System. We will have small cities on the Moon, several colonies on Mars, bases on the largest asteroids, even space stations around Jupiter and Saturn. We will have nowhere left to go—except the stars.

MOONBASE

The Apollo progams of the 1960s and 70s showed that we can work on the Moon for short periods, but a proper lunar base is needed to learn more about our nearest space neighbor. From the base, astronomers will study the sky, and doctors make new medicines.

MARS BASE

The first missions to Mars will study the surface and collect samples, but later crews will take the first sections of a Martian base. Some ten years after the first landing, there will be a team of a dozen astronauts living on Mars; ten years later the number could be ten times that.

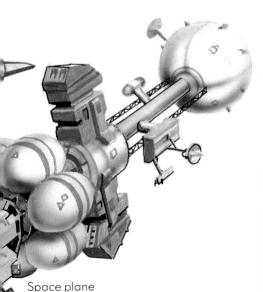

Space plane

When interstellar flight finally becomes feasible, journeys will still take years rather than days or months.

ET/UFO's

UFOs—Unidentified Flying Objects—are believed by many to be the spacecraft of alien lifeforms, first reported by a pilot who saw ''flying saucer-like objects'' in the late 1950s. But the most common sighting is still of a craft with a spinning dome and bumps on the sides. Some are hoaxes, but others cannot simply be explained away...

Many people who claim to have seen UFOs also claim to have seen the strange alien beings which pilot them. Some are huge and hairy, others very small like dwarfs; some speak English, and others an amazing alien tongue. Some witnesses say they were taken into the aliens' spaceship for medical examinations or a space journey!

The world of science fiction has given us many aliens. Perhaps, out there in space, there really are aliens like these…

The Daleks are Dr. Who's arch enemies. The protective metal casings contain jelly-like creatures called Kaleds.

E.T.—The Extra Terrestrial—was left stranded on Earth by his spaceship. He eventually returned home safely.

The alien from the film Alien was covered in spines, with razor-sharp teeth and sharp claws—and was almost indestructible.

If aliens really do exist, how they will look when we find them will depend on what sort of a planet they come from. The human shape reflects the nature of the Earth's atmosphere and environment and the strength of its gravity. Other planets have different conditions.

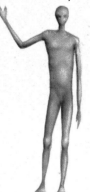

Lifeforms on a planet with a strong gravitational pull will be squashed toward the ground. They might have huge, leathery feet.

On a low gravity planet the aliens' bones would be able to grow and grow, possibly reaching 16 feet tall.

Some astronomers think that Jupiter's swirling clouds might contain ray-like creatures, with leathery wings.

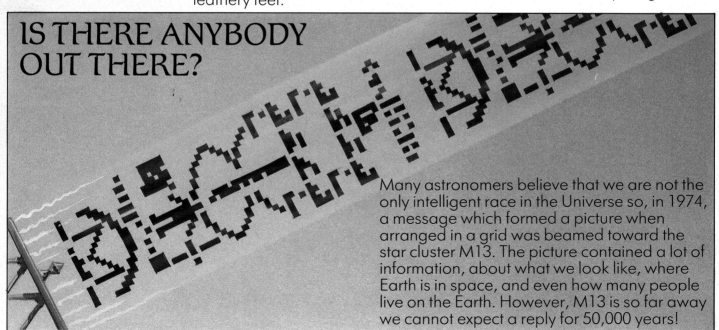

IS THERE ANYBODY OUT THERE?

Many astronomers believe that we are not the only intelligent race in the Universe so, in 1974, a message which formed a picture when arranged in a grid was beamed toward the star cluster M13. The picture contained a lot of information, about what we look like, where Earth is in space, and even how many people live on the Earth. However, M13 is so far away we cannot expect a reply for 50,000 years!

GLOSSARY

Artificial Satellite A mechanical object launched by a rocket from earth which orbits a natural body, such as a planet or a moon, etc.

Asterism An easily identifiable shape of stars in the night sky, such as a cross, a line, or a circle. Always as a part of a constellation.

Asteroid A small, irregular-shaped body which orbits the Sun like a miniature planet. Most lie in a belt between Mars and Jupiter.

Astronaut A man or a woman who travels beyond the Earth and into space. "Astronauts" from the U.S.S.R. are called *Cosmonauts*.

Astronomers Astronomers are scientists who study the heavens and all the objects in space, using telescopes and other equipment.

Astronomy The scientific study of all the objects in the heavens.

Atmosphere The blanket of different gases which surrounds and covers a planet or moon. It may be breathable or poisonous.

Aurora Borealis/ Australis Or *Northern Lights*: curtains of colored light which shine in the night sky above the Earth's poles, (Borealis = north, Australis = south).

Binoculars Binoculars are like two small telescopes joined together. They provide modest magnification and are very useful for sky watching.

Black Hole An object with such a strong gravitational pull that not even light rays can escape it. So this theoretical object appears completely black.

Colony In the future, permanently manned bases will be built on Mars and the Moon. They will be big enough to grow crops and feed all the inhabitants without returning to Earth.

Comet A comet has a solid nucleus of dirty ice, a gaseous coma, and two tails made out of gas released by the heat of the sun as the comet passes by.

Comet Nucleus The solid heart of a comet — a dirty iceberg which is covered in material as dark as soot — which orbits the Sun as part of the Solar System.

Constellation An area of the night sky given the name of a historical creature or character. There are 88 different constellations.

Cosmos Everything we can observe in the Universe — stars, planets, and galaxies, etc.

Crater A depression — shallow or deep — in a moon or planet's surface caused by the impact of a small body at high speed.

Docking The joining of one spacecraft to another. The Apollo craft docked with the Lunar lander, and the Soviet Soyuz spacecraft docks with the *Mir* space station.

EVA — Extra Vehicular Activity Work done by an astronaut outside his or her spaceship, either in space in an MMU or on the surface of the Moon or another planet.

Eclipse When one celestial body passes in front of another. A solar eclipse occurs when the Moon covers the Sun.

Elliptical If the orbit of a celestial body is a smooth, oval curve instead of a perfectly round circle it is said to be elliptical.

Equatorial Diameter The distance measured across the center of a planet from one side to the other.

Galaxies Galaxies are vast "islands" of many millions of stars in the dark ocean of space. Our own galaxy is called "The Milky Way."

Gas Giant A planet like Jupiter or Saturn, made mostly out of gas, which has no solid surface on which a spacecraft could land.

Geosynchronous Rotation When a satellite orbits a planet or moon at a certain height and moves at the same relative speed as the body below. It always stays above the same point on the surface.

Grand Tour The nickname given to the series of encounters made by the Voyager space probes with the outer planets of the Solar System.

Greenhouse Effect When a planet's atmosphere traps the heat of the Sun near its surface and steadily raises the surface temperature.

Lander A small manned or unmanned spacecraft which descends from orbit to set down on a planet or moon's surface.

Light Year Not a length of time, but the distance light travels in one year. It is equivalent to 5.9 million million miles.

MMU – Manned Maneuvering Unit A small jet back-pack worn by shuttle astronauts which lets them fly freely in space, often to capture damaged satellites.

Meteor A shooting star – a tiny piece of cometary debris which burns up in Earth's atmosphere. Any which survive are "meteorites."

Milky Way The Milky Way is our home galaxy, and it contains approximately 100,000 million stars. It has a spiral shape.

Natural Satellite A planet's moon in a natural orbit, as opposed to an artificial satellite which is built by people and launched by rocket.

Nebula A cloud of gas or dust. If there are stars nearby it will shine with their reflected light. If not, it will just look like a dark patch.

Nova The apparent sudden brightening of a star in the night sky. This is caused when material drawn from a companion star ignites.

OORT Cloud A theoretical shell of comets surrounding the Solar System like a bubble at a distance of approximately 1 light year.

Observatory From where an astronomer studies the night sky. It may either be a building high on a mountain or a special telescope up in orbit.

Occultation When one celestial body passes in front of another, e.g. the Moon passing in front of a star.

Orbit The path of one body around another, such as the Moon around the Earth or the Earth around the Sun.

Payload Special items such as satellites and scientific equipment which are carried into space and delivered into orbit by rockets.

Phases The apparent changes of a celestial body from a thin crescent to a full disk, such as Venus, Mercury, and our own Moon.

Planet A large, spherical body which orbits around the Sun or another star. Planets do not "shine," they reflect the Sun's light.

Quasar An incredibly luminous object of unexplained nature which appears very faint from Earth because it is very distant.

Radar Mapping A way of mapping a planet's hidden surface using radio waves sent from a spaceprobe or radio telescope to build up an image.

Radiation Radiation is made of electromagnetic waves or particles which travel through space carrying energy. Some forms are dangerous.

Radio Astronomy The study of radio waves coming from objects in the heavens, as opposed to the study of their light.

Radio Telescope A device shaped like a curved dish which collects radio waves from the heavens and allows them to be studied by astronomers.

Remote Control A spaceprobe is operated by remote control – commands are sent to it from operators back on Earth and it obeys them.

Retrograde Motion When a body like a comet moves around the Sun in the opposite direction to the Earth. Also, Venus has *retrograde rotation*, meaning that it spins from west to east, instead of east to west.

Ring System Millions of tiny moonlets circle the equators of the largest planets, forming bands or rings. Some are bright, others faint.

Rocket Rockets launch equipment and people into space. Their engines are very powerful, enough to overcome Earth's gravity.

Shepherd Moons The tiny moons which orbit outside and inside a planet's Ring System, keeping its ring particles in place.

Solar System All the bodies – planets, asteroids, comets, and moons – which orbit around our Sun. Other stars might have their own solar systems.

Space Probe A machine sent to explore a distant body with cameras and other scientific instruments controlled from Earth.

Space Station A structure of many different sections, built in orbit, where astronauts can live and work comfortably for long periods.

Spacecraft An unmanned machine sent from Earth to make measurements in space and to observe all the planets from close range.

Spaceship A manned spacecraft which carries astronauts into and through space and between the planets.

Speed of Light The fastest speed any object can have, equivalent to 186,000 miles per second.

Star A huge sphere of flaming gas sustained by internal nuclear reactions. Our own Sun is a medium-sized star.

Sun The star which lies at the center of our Solar System. It is 109 times wider than the Earth.

Sunspots Holes in the surface of the Sun caused by magnetic disturbances. They appear darker only because they show cooler gas below.

Supernova The explosive death of a massive star. This happens after it has consumed all its nuclear fuel.

Synchronous Rotation When a planet's moon takes the same time to spin once as it does to orbit its parent planet. Our Moon shows synchronous rotation so we always see the same side.

Telescope Telescopes magnify distant objects in the night sky, using lenses or mirrors to make things appear closer, bigger, and brighter.

The Big Bang Astronomers think the Universe was formed in a massive explosion – the Big Bang – 20 billion years ago. Before then there was nothing.

Universe The Universe is everything that exists around us – from insects to stars – whether it's been discovered or not!

Zero Gravity (or "weightlessness") When an object like an orbiting astronaut has no weight because he is beyond the reach of the force of gravity.

INDEX

Page numbers followed by the word *passim* indicate scattered mentions in the text.